Meatpies & MICROPHONES

Meat pies & MICROPHONES

The adventures of a football reporter

by Simon Mapletoft

Simon Mapletoft Media

ISBN: 978-0-9927078-0-4

Book Design: Claire Taylor, Watamu Design

Cover Photography: David Goff

Published by: Simon Mapletoft Media
Web: www.simonmapletoft.com
E-mail: enquiries@simonmapletoft.com

Printed and bound in the UK by CPI Group (UK) Ltd, Croydon, CR0 4YY

INTRODUCTION

I freely admit that I'm a very lucky man. Few people make a career out of pursuing their passions in life. But for the past 30 years, that's exactly what I've been doing. After my family, nothing has ever been closer to my heart than football and horse racing. Both have excited me, fascinated me, captivated me and consumed me for as long as I can remember. I played local league football (and cricket) avidly as a boy, teenager and man, and began to indulge my lifelong love for horses when I started riding ponies at the age of six. And I marvelled at the sight, sounds and smells of a real life football match, watching my local team Mansfield Town from the Field Mill terraces in those impressionable, formative years.

But, beyond playing and spectating, nothing burned into my soul more deeply than my overwhelming ambition to become a sports reporter. It was an ambition I realised quite out of the blue at the tender age of 18, when I set out on what has been a wonderful career path. How could I ever have imagined during those childhood days on the terraces that I would one day become the voice of Mansfield Town Football Club? That I would report on their trials and tribulations for the local BBC, the local weekly newspaper, and then its evening counterpart.

What's more, how on earth could I ever have imagined that, at the end of a journey that spanned two fantastic decades, fate would grant me another opportunity of a lifetime? The chance to report on my other great passion, horseracing, on national and international television. Whilst I am indeed very lucky, I've backed up my good fortune with years of hard work, determination and dedication. These days, my busy schedule as a presenter on the Sky Sports channel At The Races consumes my professional life, but football remains in my blood.

On hanging up my microphone at a football match for the final time in May 2002 to enter the exciting world of racing, I brought to an end the first part of my colourful life as a journalist and broadcaster. But the memories lived on and I pledged to myself that one day I would commit the best of them to print. The older we get, the more nostalgic we become, and recalling fond memories and experiences from the distant past at times pre-occupies me. So here we are. Eleven years later, my most inspiring stories and amusing anecdotes have been lovingly collected to share with those who, like myself, have dedicated much of their lives to the team that plays in amber and blue.

I didn't want this book to focus entirely on me and my own achievements. That would be boring, and rather self-indulgent. Each and every stage of my sporting and professional life has revolved around a myriad of colourful characters that shaped me, influenced me and made an impression on me in some way. I've tried to bring those characters back to life through the chapters of this book, from my school days as a budding sportsman, to my formative years in journalism and, ultimately, my two decades behind the scenes at Field Mill. I share with you the great days, and the worst days, the highs and the lows. My aim at the outset was to create an essentially light-hearted, humorous journey back through time. And in doing so, I hope that I will provoke many personal memories in many of you of those heady days at Field Mill and of Nottinghamshire sport in the Seventies, Eighties and Nineties.

Simon Mapletoft
2013

CONTENTS

CHAPTER 1

FOOTBALL IN MY BLOOD

My heart thumping against my rib cage, I dropped my left shoulder and slipped past a defender's despairing lunge. Then, pushing the ball into open space, I sprinted, breathless, before drawing back my left leg and crashing a bullet-like shot goalwards from outside the box. In an instant, it streaked above the goalkeeper's outstretched arm and dipped beneath the crossbar, bulging the back of the net. Goal! Eyes wide and screaming my delight, I turned and ran, my admiring team mates in hot pursuit. I ran and I ran and I ran. For that moment, time stood still, my bellowing cheeks as red as my Arsenal-style shirt. I had just scored my first ever goal for the junior school team, and the feeling was overwhelming. Forty years on, and that mental video clip remains crisp and vivid.

I admit my description of that unstoppable blockbuster may be a little 'Roy of the Rovers'. Only a little! But, hey, it was my first ever goal in a real life football match, and I was only nine, so I'm not going to apologise for employing a little bit of journalistic license. Playing on the left wing for Birklands Primary School in Warsop, a close-knit mining community in North Nottinghamshire, was the stuff of dreams. And throughout that school season, I just couldn't stop scoring. Crashing long-range shots over tiny goalies with my trusted left foot was a winning formula, and, thanks in no small part to my new-found exploits, our team went on an exciting cup run.

In sporting circles, the passage of time has a habit of glorifying teams and events of yesteryear, but the decades that followed certainly proved that the Birklands school team certainly wasn't short of talented, budding sportsmen. In goal was one of my best mates at the time, Neil French, who went on to be a cricketer of some repute. I'll talk some more about 'Frenchy' in a later chapter. Then there was midfield dynamo Steve Herbert, or 'Gnasher', as he was affectionately known (though I never understood why ...). He, too, went on to enjoy success as a prominent local cricketer as you will also discover in due course. Dougie Etches, fast and skilful, was an undisputable choice for team captain.

Dougie was also the hot favourite in the line-up when I took my chance in a trial race for a place at the local schools' athletics finals. Determined to make the team at the coveted Dukeries Schools' Championships in the village of New Ollerton – yet another mining community – I positioned myself prominently in a bunch start and streaked clear at the sound of the starter's whistle to claim victory, with Dougie breathing down my neck. I acquitted myself well at the finals and would almost certainly have won the dash but for mistaking the winning line and easing down yards from the designated finish. Still, taking home a certificate for third place ranked as a proud enough achievement.

The Birklands football team was honed into a cohesive unit by sports master Mr Fareham, a small, mild mannered chap who wore spectacles and a tweed jacket and did nothing but encourage gently from the touchline. In truth, his every instruction seemed to be drowned out by more than one over-enthusiastic parent. It was a huge privilege for me to slip on that red and white jersey and my moulded-stud 'Power' boots with their striking white flash, and I would count down the days from one match to the next.

However, any illusions I might have had about one day becoming a proper footballer like my idol Peter Lorimer, the Leeds United and Scotland star of the day, were soon put into harsh perspective when we met Newlands from the nearby village of Clipstone in the quarter-final of the Mansfield & District Junior Schools' Cup. To call them a one-man team would not have done them justice – they were a big, strong and quick outfit - but one player at the heart of their midfield seemed to tower over the rest of us both physically and technically. His name was Raymond Walker, who was rumoured to be interesting professional clubs even at that age. His Newlands, in their blue and white Queen's Park Rangers hoops, imposed their all-round superiority and beat us 4-1 on our own patch. The cup dream was abruptly over.

The mining village of Clipstone where Walker grew up had already produced the great Gordon Cowans, whose silky skills earned him a career at the highest level with European Cup and League Championship winners Aston Villa, as well as 10 full England caps, of course. The son of a miner, Cowans was raised on the Garibaldi Estate like so many of his young peers. Some years later, in 1982 to be precise, Walker followed Cowans to Villa Park, becoming a midfielder of great potential. He didn't quite fulfil that early promise at the highest level, but was good enough to enjoy a long and fruitful career with Port Vale, playing well over 400 times for the Potteries club following 23 run-outs for Villa. Indeed, it was the midfield partnership he forged with Robbie Earle that fired John Rudge's team to promotion from the Third Division in 1989, but Walker may be best remembered for that FA Cup fourth round goal he scored against Tottenham Hotspur that clinched his team a shock 2-1 scalp.

Further research reveals that North Shields-born Walker was twice Player of the Year at Vale Park, and appeared in the PFA Team of the Year for both the old Second and Third Divisions between 1988 and 1993. He was held in high enough regard at Port Vale to be given a testimonial game that ended in an 8-6 defeat by Leicester City! Walker, a product of Nottingham Boys, was associated with non-leaguers Leek Town and Newcastle Town at the end of his career before becoming Football in the Community Officer for Crewe Alexandra. In the first of a lifetime of sporting ironies, we were again involved in the same match some years after that schools' cup tie when he was playing professionally and I was reporting on the action from the press box.

Clipstone, in the shadows of what are believed to be the largest pit headstocks in Britain, was renowned for honing sporting talent and also laid claim to the Saxby brothers, Mick and Gary. Both enjoyed good careers in professional football, starting at Mansfield Town before going their separate ways. Mick, a tall centre-half with a mop of curly hair, made his debut for the Stags at 18 and became the subject of a club record transfer fee of around £200,000 (involving Hatters striker Steve Taylor) when he signed for Luton Town in 1979. He secured another notable move, this time to Middlesbrough in 1984 before injury ended his career. A popular figure among the local sporting fraternity, 'Sax' had a spell as commercial manager with Mansfield and also worked as a summariser on the local radio station Mansfield 103.2 – a role he still performs from time to time.

Younger brother Gary was a different type of footballer. Smaller and quicker, he blossomed into a reliable midfielder, but needed a move to Northampton Town in 1980 to establish himself after being unable to break into the Stags first team. Gary remained in local football, managing Ashfield United in the early Nineties and was also a talented cricketer, turning out for Glapwell and also Clipstone Colliery in the top flight of the nationally renowned Bassetlaw League. Alongside him was Andy Pick, who became brother-in-law to another famous Clipstone son David Millns. Pick took almost 500 first class wickets for Nottinghamshire between 1983 and 1997, while strike bowler Millns topped the 500-wicket mark during his distinguished career with Notts and Leicestershire. At this juncture I should also mention Robbie Sprigg, a reliable all-rounder who was as effective on the cricket pitch as he was as a footballer. Robbie looked after the Clipstone Colliery turf for a number of years before working as the groundsman at Mansfield's Field Mill.

Unlike Walker's, my footballing aspirations sadly took a sudden downturn the year after that schools' cup defeat when I arrived full of hope and expectation for a trial for the first year footie team at the Meden Comprehensive. Being the star winger for Birklands, I was sure to claim my place, I figured, despite competition from the best players from other neighbouring primary schools, but the chance of showing off my (lethal) left foot quickly passed me by in the strangest of circumstances. There must have been 50 similar hopefuls congregated on the school field after class that day, all keen to catch the sports master's eagle eye. But the shambles that followed didn't exactly bode well for the Meden's prospects in the senior schools' cup that year. To my dismay, I found myself lost among a mass scrimmage when the teacher kicked a ball high in the air and commanded us all - en masse - to give chase. Then, at random, he singled out those fortunate to be close enough to kick it (and therefore show some level of ability) before declaring the 'trial' over.

There would be no number 11 shirt for me at the 'big' school, and being quite a shy, retiring kid at that age, I wasn't inclined to kick up any sort of fuss. So, disillusioned, I contented myself with jumpers-for-posts kick-abouts with my mates after school. Like many boys of my age, I was, quite simply, football mad. Back in the Seventies we had no computers, no PlayStations, no Nintendo Wii games to distract us from endless hours of exercise and fresh air. Every spare minute was spent kicking a ball, and by the time the park keeper locked the gates each night in the gathering gloom, the goals tally had escalated into a rugby score.

In those days, it seemed that everyone in the playground supported either Leeds United, Liverpool or Manchester United, the top teams of the era. My allegiance, as you will have already gathered by my reference to Lorimer, was to Leeds. The Revie era had reached its dominant peak when Leeds were crowned First Division Champions at the end of the 1973-74 season, but by the time I made my first ever pilgrimage to Elland Road on 1st March 1975, those glory days were already behind them. Revie was now in charge of the England team, Clough's well-documented 44-day reign had been and gone, and now it was up to Jimmy Armfield to revive the club's faltering fortunes.

Revie's legacy was, in a boy's eyes, still very much in evidence. Reaney, Hunter and Madeley were still lynchpins of the defence, while the diminutive Bremner held together the midfield. Up front, the goalscoring prowess of Allan Clarke and Mick Jones offered hope, and my idol Lorimer was still rocketing those exocets past helpless goalies from all angles.

So, Leeds were taking on Manchester City, and there I was – home-knitted club scarf knotted proudly around my right wrist – making my way up the stadium steps with my equally excited parents. Emerging at the top of the concourse conjures memories that will stay with me forever. The deafening buzz of a 47,489 crowd, the vivid red asphalt framing a lush green pitch, that intoxicating aroma of cigar smoke and Bovril, and the strains of Steve Harley and Cockney Rebel's 'Come Up And See Me (Make Me Smile)' resonating beneath the grandstands. We stood almost directly behind the goal, closer than a penalty kick to David Harvey's posts. Lorimer, crafting clever passes from around the box in his resplendent white jersey, was, at times, within touching distance it seemed. The game ended in a 2-2 draw with my hero scoring both goals. Not quite the result we hoped for but an unforgettable experience for this fledgling football fan.

As I said, my football life is punctuated with ironies, and some years later I would work alongside the then Leeds boss Armfield in a live radio broadcast at Turf Moor, Burnley, when the former manager was established as a front line reporter for BBC Radio Five Live. Little did I realise, too, that I would be describing the action on live radio at Elland Road when Leeds slipped on a big yellow banana skin against Mansfield in the League Cup almost 20 years later.

Lorimer's number seven sat proudly on my own back at Christmas 1974 when I ripped away the wrapping paper to reveal a crisp white Leeds strip, complete with the little blue pennant-style sock numbers. Remember them? Some time later, I also got the yellow away kit (with the blue and white stripes on the sleeves) that was flying off the shelves at Packer Sports in Mansfield like those proverbial hot cakes. However, the white of Leeds wasn't my first replica kit, and neither was Lorimer my first footballing idol. At a much younger age (about five I think) I could be found toe-poking my football around the back garden in the white

Mansfield kit of the day. I adored it. A white shirt with a blue and yellow trim; blue shorts and white socks, complete with blue and yellow hoops.

This time my hero was another number seven, the one and only Malcolm Partridge. His exploits on the wing captivated me even at that early age. I can vaguely recall perching on my Dad's shoulders on the old West Stand terraces when Malcolm was making a name for himself with 13 goals in 39 appearances in the 1969-70 season. Looking back at the record books, I discovered that the Chesterfield-born forward made his Stags debut at the tender age of just 17. Leicester City were impressed enough to fork out £50,000 for him in September 1970 (a substantial fee in those days) and he went on to help them secure the Second Division title. Some years later, Malcolm's son Scott Partridge made a successful career in the game for a string of clubs including Bristol City, Cardiff City, Torquay United and Brentford.

Wintry Saturday afternoons on Mansfield's Field Mill terraces remain among my fondest early childhood memories. There was nothing quite like a match day. The first sight of the imposing West Stand as we approached from the car park; the click of those heavy metal turnstiles; that heady cocktail of cigar smoke and Bovril; the theatre provided by the familiar strains of the latest vinyls spun through the crackles of the public address system, courtesy of Sid Booth's record store in town; and the anticipation stirred by the infectious 'On The Ball' theme the players ran out to at five to three.

The thud of leather upon leather as players lashed at the ball only feet beyond the concrete wall in front of us was mesmerising; and the sudden roar of the crowd packed tightly around us, punctuated by the shrill invasion of a wooden rattle, was equally contagious. Watching The Stags became an essential part of family life by the mid-Seventies, and soon my parents and I were up in the West Stand seats each week, screaming our delight as quicksilver winger Jimmy McCaffrey whipped over an unrelenting supply of pinpoint crosses for Terry Eccles and Ray Clarke to head into the roof of the North Stand net. On reflection, they really were golden times. Leeds had won the First Division title in 1974, and a year later The Stags became Division Four Champions under Dave Smith. By 1977, my local club had won promotion to the old Second Division for the first time in their history, this time under the leadership of the popular Peter Morris. Football had me well and truly hooked: playing it, watching it, listening to it and even writing about it. Though embryonic, my destiny was taking shape.

Digression: In parallel to my love for football, I was also pursuing my other lifelong passion for horses at this time. From the age of six, I was fortunate enough to own my own ponies – three in succession – that were kept on a small holding in the village. Mum and Dad must have spent every spare, hard-earned penny on this pursuit and it was an interest I would maintain into my early teens, when other sporting interests took priority. Picking up where I left off, I returned to the saddle as a competitive rider in my late Twenties and then, a decade later, dedicated my career to the most magnificent of all equines: the racehorse. For now, though, lets concentrate on football.

CHAPTER 2

LIVE FROM THE SUBBUTEO STADIUM

From the night I was allowed to stay up late at a very young age and watch Leeds United versus Manchester United on Match of the Day on my Auntie Annie's new colour telly (ours was only black and white), watching and writing about football fascinated me. I can still picture that image of the great George Best in glorious technicolour, weaving in between defenders in his scarlet shirt. By the time I had reached my early teens, immersing myself in a big game on television became a highlight. Of course, back in the Seventies live football wasn't anywhere near as accessible as it is today – no Sky Sports in those days - so a game on the box was a real treat.

Whilst watching the action, I would often feel compelled to get out my best ballpoint pen and write my own match report, describing the drama and excitement of what I had just witnessed. Perhaps it was an overwhelming desire to somehow be more closely involved in what was unfolding on the screen. To be a part of it all. Whatever my motivation may have been, it turned out to be very good practice. I would also spend hours stretched out on the lounge carpet flicking my Subbuteo heroes around a green felt pitch. My favourite teams would go head to head in front of the gas fire, which illuminated the baize like floodlights. Often I would create a match programme, complete with pen pictures and team lists, and would fill notepads full of statistics from my many games. The 'Championship Manager' generation may have enjoyed a much more virtual experience, but there was something wonderful about getting lost in one's own imagination as a youngster.

Buying a new Subbuteo team in its distinctive green and white box from the long gone Linney's store in Mansfield town centre was very exciting. Each box cost 50p, and occasionally I would add some extras to my collection, like a grandstand, a referee or a handful of supporters. Like many of today's real life stars, the Subbuteo men were fragile, and the occasional unexpected pitch invasion by the dog had me reaching for the super glue. I even rubbed soil into the goalmouths to make the pitch look more realistic. During those long winter evenings, I would disappear deep into my own world - a world I so desperately wanted to live in, for real.

Down on the local 'rec', my mates and I would simulate big games in front of full sized goalposts in our respective replica kits. We'd have big local derbies, cup finals and World Cups, with my commentaries as the backdrop. My descriptive narratives spilled out of me almost instinctively, and I think it's fair to say that our games certainly wouldn't have seemed quite so exciting without them. My collection of match reports, complete with blockbusting headlines, went upmarket when my Mum and Dad bought me a gleaming new typewriter one Christmas in my early teens. I amassed volumes of mythical reports, more of those homemade match programmes and fictional league tables. A highlight of pre-season for me was to rush down to the local newsagent's and buy Shoot magazine, complete with those colourful cardboard league ladders for all four divisions. Moving the tabs up and down the ladder according to each team's points tally was a weekend highlight.

'Match of the Day', the big games on ITV and the regional Sunday 'Soccer' programme on Yorkshire Television were simply unmissable and I engrossed myself in the contrasting styles of commentating icons John Motson, Barry Davies, the late Brian Moore, Martin Tyler, John Helm - and even the late Keith Macklin. Remember him? Yorkshire Television's coverage was particularly compelling as it would offer the opportunity to see the local clubs in action. Seeing Mansfield on telly seemed almost unbelievable!

Macklin punctuated those Sunday afternoon highlights with his own inimitable, northern brogue. He was quite simply the voice of Yorkshire football from 1969 to 1976 and even found his way onto ITV's commentary team for the 1974 World Cup Finals in Germany. Macklin's successor was a 31-year-old Tyler, who soon emerged as number two to ITV kingpin Moore en route to a long distinguished career with Sky Sports, of course. Having admired his commentaries as a boy, I had the great pleasure of meeting Martin on several occasions some years later when I became a football commentator myself. His replacement on ITV was John Helm, a born and bred Yorkshireman whose party piece was to rattle off the names of all 92 Football League clubs in 26 seconds flat. He was also a very good commentator, and, as I discovered when our paths crossed professionally, a true gentleman.

As I pointed out, football on television wasn't anywhere near as accessible in those days, but I got just as much pleasure out of pressing my ear against our transistor radio to marvel at the sublime descriptions of the BBC's inimitable Peter Jones as they emerged through the persistent crackles. Jones was, quite simply, my role model, as he added colour and theatre to all the big midweek games on 'Sport On Two' alongside the likes of Bryon Butler and Mike Ingham. Welsh-born Jones possessed an enviable command of the English language, delivered in intoxicating tones. His ability to conjure vivid pictures in the listener's mind was unrivalled and it was a sad day when he passed away in 1990 after collapsing during commentary of the Boat Race. His BBC colleague John Rawling, who, like me began his journalistic career with the Mansfield Chronicle Advertiser (lovingly known as the Chad), paid a fitting tribute when he said: "Peter was an old school charmer and an inspirational colleague for all aspiring broadcasters … In my opinion, nobody before or since has ever broadcast with greater descriptive brilliance than Peter did on the day of the Hillsborough disaster."

As John said, Jones was positively old school - one of the last of a line that in my view also included the exceptional Colin Slater, the voice of Notts County to this day. I was still dreaming of becoming a football commentator myself when Colin was gracing the airwaves for BBC Radio Nottingham. I would never meet Jones, but it was to become my great fortune to work with Colin for 13 years when I eventually fulfilled my boyhood dream in the late Eighties. In those teenage years, Wednesday mornings were as much a highlight as Sunday afternoons on the telly and those midweek nights by the radio. That was when the local paper, the Chad, would fall through the letterbox. I'd go straight to the back page, of course, to find out if legendary Mansfield Town reporter Stan Searl had been at the same Stags match as me the previous Saturday! I had no inkling back then that Stan, like Colin, would become a big influence on my early career.

CHAPTER 3

FRENCH CRICKET

Though still captivated by the beautiful game, the disappointment of not making the Meden School team refused to subside, so at the age of 13 I turned my attentions to another of my sporting passions, cricket, and established myself as a fast bowler in a school eleven assembled with much more structure and purpose than the football team ever was. Football still had so much more to offer me than I could ever have imagined, both recreationally and professionally, but this was the start of another sporting love affair. Cricket was just as much my obsession as football throughout my teens. I enjoyed the proud distinction of playing in the all-conquering Welbeck Colliery youth team until I was 18, alongside some tremendous players like Neil French – the junior school goalie and a younger brother of Nottinghamshire and England wicketkeeper Bruce French. Neil, a big lad for his age, was born into a tremendous sporting family and went on to represent his country at amateur level.

We were firm friends even before we sat at a school desk, and it wasn't long before we were staging countless Test Matches on the local 'rec' in the summer holidays. I still grin now when I think about 'Frenchy' pounding lively short-pitched deliveries at mates who wore skateboard helmets for protection. Another mate, David Goff, now a master butcher in the Sherwood Forest village of Edwinstowe, was good with a blade of a different type. He honed his batting technique on that of Nottinghamshire and England ace Derek Randall, even down to his top of the range Gunn & Moore bat. Dave even mimicked Randall's fidgety style at the crease, and from the boundary ropes only his mop of red hair distinguished him from his hero.

So keen we were that the friendly park keeper used to mow us a fresh strip of grass for a wicket, deep in the outfield. As obliging as he was, it would have been more than his job was worth to allow us to tread on the carefully manicured square at the council-run Carr Lane sports ground in Warsop, though we did have a whip round to hire it one sunbaked afternoon. The anticipation of a proper innings on a proper pitch clearly got the better of me as I was sent back to the pavilion having scored only one run. Another regular venue for a big Test was the driveway at Neil's house, just around the corner from mine on the adjoining council estate. On occasions, big brother Bruce would join in, too. The old metal dustbin was the wicket, a thick edge onto the coalhouse door was a slip catch, and a six over the neighbour's fence was 'out'.

Neil went on to captain our school team and the youth team at Welbeck

Colliery, a widely respected club in the prominent Bassetlaw League, run by his father Maurice French. Young 'Frenchy' was a no-nonsense all-rounder in the Ian Botham mould. He was the fourth of five sons raised by Maurice and Betty, who were responsible for probably the greatest sporting dynasty in the county. Their second son Charlie almost made the breakthrough into first class cricket himself with Nottinghamshire in the Seventies. A prolific opening batsman, he captained Welbeck's first eleven for many years as well as representing the Nottinghamshire Cricket Association, and was widely acknowledged as one of the best opening batsmen in the Bassetlaw League and beyond. He was another role model during my summers as an aspiring cricketer, so how ironic it was again that some years later, in my capacity as sports editor of my local paper the Chad, we would renew our association. Charlie would work for me as a rugby correspondent, of all things. Aside from cricket, he loved the 15-man game and was also a talented amateur footballer. Through the paper, I also helped him publicise his embryonic cricket bat manufacturing venture, which I'm delighted to see has developed into a thriving business today. CF Sports manufactures and sells a range of sporting clothing and equipment from its Mansfield Woodhouse base in North Nottinghamshire.

Oldest brother Joe, and the youngest, David, were also excellent with bat and ball and both contributed to Welbeck's dominance in the Bassetlaw League before the club became a founder member of the Notts Premier League. Bruce, meanwhile, was the real star of the all-conquering French family. How exciting it was to see my mate's older brother – the kid who hoisted my misplaced deliveries over countless garden fences - donning the wicketkeeper's gloves in Test Matches on the telly. He made his first class debut for Nottinghamshire as a 16-year-old in 1976, and was a regular the following summer when Mike Harris gave up the gloves to concentrate on scoring much-needed runs. Because of the dominance of Kent's Alan Knott and Derbyshire's Bob Taylor through the next decade, Bruce had to wait until 1986 to make his Test debut for England, against India at Headingley. He went on to play in 16 Tests and 13 one-day internationals, taking 38 catches. He also proved useful with the bat against Pakistan in 1987 when he battled his way to an invaluable half-century in a rain-affected drawn match. But for the stature of Knott and Taylor, and a series of injuries in the late Eighties, Bruce would surely have made many more Test appearances.

Maurice himself lived for cricket. Always so modest about his sons' achievements, he worked tirelessly to drive Welbeck forward, and was just as happy rolling the wicket and cutting the grass as he was taking charge of the club's administration. Maurice sadly passed away a few years ago, and the wickets he tended so meticulously at the club's long-standing Oakfield Lane home in Warsop have been bulldozed beneath a new housing estate, but his legacy certainly lives on now that Welbeck have found a new purpose-built home a few miles away. The man who provided that home was prominent local businessman John Fretwell, who had the Sookholme complex purpose built after selling his cash and carry business for millions early in the new Millennium. John, a self-made man and a pillar of his local community, started his working life cutting hair in a barber's shop in Warsop. He was the first hairdresser to take a pair of scissors to my tiny head as a toddler, and in later years shared my love for horse racing. Like me, John went on to own a string of winning thoroughbreds, though on a much bigger scale than my budgets allowed.

While Bruce was establishing himself as the best young wicketkeeper in the country, Neil and I were playing our part in establishing Welbeck as a dominant force in the old Portland Youth League. Without doubt, my finest moment was opening the batting in our double-winning season against a very strong Worksop side at Central Avenue, back in 1981. It was the first time I had opened the innings, and nerves almost got the better of me. In truth, I was fortunate to remain at the crease after forcing a succession of thick edges between the leaping slips. But remain I did, putting on a century stand with my fellow opener Steve Antcliffe before finally succumbing to a tired swing just three short of my 50. Our knock made the headlines in the sports pages of the Worksop Guardian, and I still have the cutting. It was my first big innings with my new bat, a Stuart Surridge Jumbo. As cricket bats went, it was a little on the heavy side with its chunky blade, but after watching in awe on television as the great West Indian Viv Richards lashed the England attack with his, I simply had to have one.

That innings clinched me a first team call up, back at Central Avenue, just a week or two later. Chances to impress were limited, but it was an amazing thrill to be in the same dressing room as the cricketers I had championed almost as much as the great Test stars who inspired me so much on television. Nottinghamshire fast bowler Kevin Cooper and West Indian international Nirmal Nanan often made appearances in a team that would have held its own with any county side. I fielded attentively and efficiently, but must confess to being clean bowled by a wily old leg spinner after managing to fend off only a handful of deliveries.

By now our youth team had won the Portland Youth League, and were poised to take on the champions of another youth competition in a 'Champion of Champions' face off at Blyth Cricket Club near Worksop. There was no starring role for me this time, but after a solid display in the field against Kiveton Park I was happy to collect my medal at the end of the game when the double had been clinched in style. Steve Herbert, a team mate in that junior school football team, was also a recipient.

Hungry for action, and by now a regular in Welbeck seconds, I combined my Bassetlaw League appearances with regular games for another local team, Warsop Workingmen's Club, who operated in the lower yet fiercely competitive Mansfield and District League. Andy Kowalski, a midfielder with Chesterfield, was a regular, too. I had followed Andy's football career with great interest after watching him graduate from Welbeck Colliery's youth team around 1970, a side managed by my Dad's workmate John Deller. Interestingly, Nottingham Forest and Chesterfield defender John Cottam played in the same team. Andy went on to play football for

England Boys' Clubs in 1970-71 and established himself as a reliable midfielder with The Spireites, scoring over 30 goals in around 400 appearances. He moved on to Doncaster Rovers, helping them achieve promotion in 1984, before finishing his career with a spell at Peterborough United and another back at Saltergate.

Another team mate at Warsop was Mansfield Town midfielder Noel Parkinson, who was as enthusiastic on the cricket square as he was on the football pitch. A bubbly character who lit up the dressing room, Noel simply loved his sport and it was a great thrill for a teenager to be able to call himself a team mate of two professional footballers. Noel, you might recall, began his career with Ipswich Town and arrived at Field Mill in 1980 for a well spent £35,000. Popular for his industrious approach, he gave two years service to The Stags before moving on to Scunthorpe United, and helping them emerge from the doldrums of the old Fourth Division alongside good old pros like Joe Neenan, Steve Baines and Steve Cammack. After hanging up his boots, Noel reported on The Iron for a local radio station and it was great to renew the acquaintance in the Glanford Park press box when I became a football commentator myself a decade or more after those summer weekends on the cricket field. It's great to see that these days Noel has enjoyed tremendous success in the online motor sales business.

Cricket at Mansfield League level may not have enjoyed the stature of the Bassetlaw game, but no quarter was even given, and there was no special dispensation for a minor either, I can assure you. I still have some old cinefilm of me, aged about 14, fending off a succession of whirlwind deliveries from New Hucknall Colliery's imposing fast bowler Steve Ogrizovic on a wicket that wasn't without a divot or two. Oggy, better known as Coventry City's FA Cup winning goalkeeper, seemed to almost disappear beyond the sightscreen before launching himself towards the return crease to pound the seam of a new ball into the face of my bat.

Mansfield-born Steve, whose younger brother Alan played cricket for Welbeck, was born in Mansfield, and turned out for New Hucknall in between appearances for Minor Counties side Shropshire. Although he didn't have the satisfaction of taking my wicket at Carr Lane that day, he did enjoy the distinction of removing Test players Chris Broad, Martyn Moxon and Alvin Kallicharran in NatWest Trophy and Benson & Hedges Cup games. As a goalkeeper, 'Oggy' made over 600 professional appearances in a career spanning 23 seasons (1977-2000). After five years as understudy at Liverpool, he joined Shrewsbury Town for a couple of seasons before making the first of more than 500 appearances for the Sky Blues, including that magnificent Wembley triumph in 1987. My research also reveals the giant 'keeper is also one of only four players to have performed at the top flight of English football in four different decades. Peter Shilton, John Lukic and Sir Stanley Matthews are the others.

Like 'Oggy', I was also combining football with cricket, albeit at a much lower level, but my passion for pursuing both sports ultimately cost me my place in the Welbeck seconds. It was etiquette in those days, as it probably still is, to see out the football season before swapping your shin pads for your cricket pads. Similarly, the summer game would take priority over football commitments come the autumn. But when I had to miss Welbeck Second Eleven's first game of the season to play football for a club I had formed myself, new captain Roy Hunt took exception. Having been carefully honed by Welbeck since the age of 13, and looking forward to establishing myself as a successful contributor at senior level, I was gutted by rugged veteran Roy's reaction. In his hasty disapproval, he failed to acknowledge my long-standing commitment to my club, and the game, and reluctantly, aged 19, I chose to move on, feeling rather wounded.

Welcoming me were fellow Bassetlaw Leaguers Thoresby Park Cricket Club, who played their home games against the beautiful backdrop of the historic Thoresby Hall, near Clumber Park, in the days before Warners turned it into a holiday destination. I spent three or four seasons with the club, run seamlessly by a true gentleman Gordon Beastall and his committee, and enjoyed my cricket immensely. The highlight was not an unbeaten stint at the crease, nor an economic haul of wickets, but a spectacular run out with just one stump to aim at from deep mid-on. It may have been more luck than judgement, but it remains filed in my mind's own video library along with that first goal for the school team. However, appearances became fewer and further between as my career as a sports journalist began to take root.

Digression: Welbeck Colliery Cricket Club was a big part of my youth so it was a great honour to be asked to attend one of their end-of-season presentation evenings some years later as guest of honour in my capacity at Chad sports editor. Even though I had hung up my spikes, my weekly reports on the local cricket scene had kept me in touch with the players I had grown up with.

CHAPTER 4

VIEW FROM THE BRIDGE

As a sports mad teenager, I enjoyed watching almost as much as playing. One of the most inspiring aspects of following professional cricket as an impressionable boy in the Seventies was the accessibility of the players, in that most grew up in the county they represented. Unlike in top flight football, home grown players became true local icons, and many could even be seen playing local league cricket when time permitted. Watching the professional game was a highlight of many a summer holiday and trips to Trent Bridge to support Nottinghamshire and Queens Park in Chesterfield to see Derbyshire in action were always exciting. A cheese sandwich, a bottle of pop and a handful of Mum's loose change for bus fare was all that was needed for a great day out in the sunshine.

Central Avenue in Worksop was also a familiar venue, as each summer, my mates and I would watch Nottinghamshire perform in the County Championship. It was an intimate setting for a professional game, and mingling with the stars in front of the pavilion wasn't discouraged. In fact, getting Geoff Boycott's autograph on the pavilion steps in 1979 was a proud moment. Nottinghamshire were on the cusp of their glory days when they hosted Yorkshire in July of that year but records remind me how they paid the ultimate price for dismissing the great Boycott for only two runs in Yorkshire's first innings. A buzz of disbelief circled the ground, I recall, and Yorkshire suffered the indignity of having to follow on, but Sir Geoffrey single-handedly made a match of it when he exacted his revenge with a stunning unbeaten innings of 175. It was unforgettable.

However, another undefeated knock, this time by Nottinghamshire's young cavalier from Retford, Derek Randall, ensured a local victory. 'Rags' had reached his half-century when the Yorkshire total was passed, but the defining moment for me was a swashbuckling innings by his team mate John Birch on the opening day. 'Birchy', entering the fray at number six, took full advantage of a docile wicket by amassing a magnificent 94 not out. Yorkshire's bewildered attack including Chris Old, Steve Oldham and Geoff Cope was demoralised as the stocky Birch hoisted boundary upon boundary over the Central Avenue ropes. And boy did we cheer as several short-pitched deliveries were dispatched high into the Worksop canal for a whopping six.

Further research confirms that Birch, from Aspley, played first class cricket for his county for 15 years between 1973 and 1988. He went on to both captain and manage the team and was awarded his county cap in 1981 before being granted a benefit eight years later. I got to know John and several other Notts players well during my early reporting years and admired his dedication to the county badge. At the end of his Nottinghamshire career, Birch pursued his cricketing passion just for fun with local clubs such as Papplewick in the early Nineties. His son Daniel Birch followed in dad's footsteps and enjoyed the distinction of making 130 on his first class debut for Derbyshire in 2007. A proud achievement.

On the same team sheet as Birch, Randall and, of course, French behind the stumps in that Nottinghamshire team of 1979 were the great Clive Rice and Eddie Hemmings, as well as county stalwarts Paul Todd, Mike Harris, Trevor Tunnicliffe and Pete Hacker. A left-arm medium-pacer from Lenton, Hacker also played for Derbyshire before plying his trade in Minor Counties cricket, and provided me with one of my most amusing memories of Sunday League cricket at The Bridge. Fielding deep on the boundary one barmy afternoon, Hacker swallowed an impressive catch and proceeded to hold the ball aloft in triumph to a packed stand, not realising that the umpire had called a no-ball. The more the home fans screamed to alert him, the more he milked their applause with his back to play, whilst the grateful batsmen scampered between the wickets to sneak a couple of extra runs. When Peter eventually got the message, his cheeks must have been as red as the ball he had been proudly caressing.

Randall, an unassuming ball of nervous energy, had emerged from the realms of Bassetlaw League club Retford, and marvelling at his performances in endless Test matches gave me almost as much pleasure as following the burgeoning career of local boy made good, Bruce French. Derek's defining moment was that epic 174 against the Aussies in the Centenary Test in Melbourne in 1977. And many of you will recall how the jumpy little fidget infuriated the raging Dennis Lillee by doffing his cap to him after a vicious bouncer, and then climbing back to his feet to salute the legendary pace man after being floored by another killer delivery. My most stirring personal memory of Randall, however, was the incident that brought a sudden hush to Trent Bridge in the summer of 1977 when Boycott ran out the local hero early in England's first innings against Australia in the Third Test. It was a shocking misjudgement by the great opening batsman, one which deprived the clown prince of the chance to make a memorable impact on his home soil. In his defence, Boycott did go some way to redeeming himself by picking his way to a century before succumbing to the great Jeff Thomson.

I took my seat at a packed Trent Bridge in the summer of 1983 hoping to see Randall put the record straight in front of his own adoring supporters following a six-year wait – and none of us was disappointed. Batting down the order in the Fourth Test against New Zealand's Kiwis, Retford's finest crashed 83 off 116 balls and looked destined to reach his century until another of Nottinghamshire's most famous sons, Richard Hadlee, ended his two and a half-hour stay at the crease.

My first ever visit to Trent Bridge was on a school trip in July 1978, when David Lloyd and Lancashire were the visitors for a Schweppes County Championship clash. The Nottinghamshire side was packed with home-produced talent: Skegby-born Tim Robinson, Birch and, behind the stumps French, whose younger brother Neil was sitting close by me on the Bridgford End terrace. For the record, an amazing double century by captain fantastic Clive Rice had put the visitors well and truly to the sword and Rice and the ever-reliable Kevin Cooper soon had them following on. However, a defiant 185 by Lloyd rescued a draw.

Some years later it would be my privilege to meet Robinson on a number of occasions in my job as Chad's sports editor and reporter for BBC Radio Nottingham. There were many column inches to be filled from Tim's exploits both for Nottinghamshire and for England. A closer look at his record proves him to be one of Ashfield's greatest sporting sons. He played in 425 first class matches, scoring over 27,000 runs and amassing 63 centuries. His international career spanned 29 Test Matches.

Back in the late Seventies, Kent were the Leeds United of the county scene and I revelled in watching them dispatch their John Player League opposition on BBC2 on Sunday afternoons. Opening batsman Chris Tavare, the cultured Pakistan all-rounder Asif Iqbal, seasoned skipper Alan Ealham, England's wicket keeper Alan Knott and towering blond fast bowler Graham Dilley were all inspirational in their own way. Such an impression they created on this budding young all-rounder that I wrote to the club for a county badge, and had it sewn proudly onto a cricket sweater my Mum knitted in the Kent livery. I can only recall seeing them 'live' on two occasions, when they took on Derbyshire in the picturesque setting of Queen's Park. Every penny of the bus ride to Chesterfield was repaid tenfold when England's Bob Woolmer smashed a fabulous century in a Schweppes County Championship game in 1979, supplemented by an entertaining 83 from Chris Cowdrey.

Two years earlier, my Kent hero Iqbal top scored in a John Player League innings with a short-lived but entertaining 32 before being trapped in the pads by England's Geoff Miller. Kent's 150 looked an easy target for the home side but they were beaten by just one run despite the heroics with the bat of tail-enders Mike Hendrick and Phil Russell. I've made the point already that I find it quite amazing and indeed a privilege that my journalistic career has brought me into contact with the heroes of my youth on so many occasions. For example, how could I have known that 12 years later I would be sat in commentary position at a football match beside the great Hendrick? That's another tale I'll save until later.

CHAPTER 5

SUNDAY MORNING DREAMERS

Once stumps had been pulled up at the end of those long teenage summers, those after-school kick-abouts in the dwindling light were sowing the seeds of my resurgent football career. And though it probably seemed a ridiculous flight of fancy at the time, I was - at the tender age of 17 - intent on somehow realising an audacious ambition to form my own football club. That way I wouldn't have to endure any more of those unfair trials and would be guaranteed a game every Sunday morning! In all seriousness, securing a game for myself wasn't the real motive. It became highly apparent that the lads who kicked that ball around with me from dawn 'til dusk every weekend were seriously good footballers – and surprisingly none of us was attached to a local youth team. So, why not give ourselves a name and become a real team? It was a challenge I couldn't resist and I would spend hours planning, anticipating and dreaming of the possibilities ahead.

Finding enough players was never going to be a problem. In fact, I didn't need to be an aspiring Sir Bobby Robson to realise there was enough talent among us to be recognised as a 'team'. We probably felt, in many ways, like those guitar wielding spotty teenagers who were out to convince anyone who would listen that they were going to be the next Iron Maiden. But, whatever I might have lacked in talent on the field, I more than made up for in ambition and determination, and this was certainly no pipe dream.

What we needed now was a kit, some fixtures - and a little bit of parental guidance. By chipping in just 10 pence per week each over a period of a few months, we had raised the princely sum of £10. The kit was easily sourced. In no time, I had followed up an advert in the local paper and acquired a set of gold second hand shirts from a pub team called the Rifle Volunteer from Skegby, near Mansfield. It wasn't until a few months later that we were able to afford to complete our team kit, thanks to a raffle that raised a further £20. These meagre funds bought us a set of new black shorts and socks from a sports shop in Mansfield. I can still remember the excitement of having 12 black numbers steam printed onto the back of our shirts, and each of us deciding which one we would wear.

By now I had become a central defender-cum midfielder, perhaps more renowned for own goals than those spectacular 20-yard strikes from the left wing. At this juncture I acquired a coaching manual by the former Manchester United manager Dave Sexton, and over the months ahead it became essential reading. Sexton, a great coach of his generation, became another role model and many of his training routines were put into practice during our regular midweek sessions. We trained hard at the council-owned Carrs Recreation Ground in Warsop that was to become our official home.

Suddenly, almost overnight in fact, we really were a football team. We looked the part, but needed to put ourselves to the test. One of our first games, a friendly against Mansfield Sunday Leaguers Vale Road United, almost ended in luckless defeat, until an injury time equaliser scraped us a 4-4 draw. We had been 3-0 down in the closing stages so deserved a share of the spoils. No doubt those yawning extra minutes that the makeshift referee - my Dad! - added on played some small part. But it was another early practice game, against our teachers at the Meden Comp, that gave me the most satisfaction. Determined to silence one or two doubters, I led my newly formed team to a memorable victory. However, it was a measure of our progress that we held Mansfield Town's under 18s to a 2-1 scoreline in a friendly at Field Mill, organised with the help of the late Stags coach Jock Basford. The game was played on the old training ground, but imagine our excitement at getting changed in the first team dressing rooms beneath the old West Stand.

In the months that followed my Dad, who at this point I should introduce to you as Dennis, stepped in as club secretary, becoming the adoptive father of another 15 sons. His role could not be overstated. He marked out the pitch, put up the nets, attended meetings and looked after all that important paperwork that I suppose would have been a less than ideal distraction from my studies. It was hard work, but Dad was a very good footballer himself in his youth (much better than I ever was, he insists) and relived it in many ways through a role he relished. Our goalkeeper's uncle, Tony Jackson, a staunch Mansfield Town supporter who worked in insurance, became an ideal choice for treasurer. Even my Mum Doreen was seconded as chief kit washer and provider of half-time oranges – a very important job indeed.

In those days, the local Sunday league – affiliated to the Nottinghamshire Football Association - boasted around 150 clubs, all marshalled by tireless secretary Ken Burgess and his hard-working committee. Apart from the top few divisions, which were graced by many top local non-league players, the standard was similar throughout. So Warsop Rangers were born, and at the start of the 1982-83 season became proud members of the Mansfield and District Sunday League Division 10! A disco had raised another £60 which paid our affiliation costs and bought us two new sets of goalpost netting. Then, Nigel Griffin – a former cricketing team mate at Warsop Workingmen's Club – very generously provided us with a gleaming new strip emblazoned with the name of his insurance company.

But why Warsop Rangers, I hear you ask? Well, most of us lived in Warsop, so that is easy to explain, but 'Rangers'... well. It turned out that half a century earlier, my Grandad had also been involved in a local football club of the same name, and resurrecting it seemed like a good idea. We even got a write-up in the local

Warsop News, with a team photo printed alongside a snap shot of the original Rangers, circa 1930. We were team mates on the pitch, and great mates off it. And that, in essence, was a secret of our success. As Sunday league teams go, we did look the part. No beer bellies, knee bandages or odd coloured socks in this team! We were all young, slim and fit and up for the challenge. The names on the team sheet conjure fond memories of some great lads who, three decades on, have gone their separate ways. It's a pity that so many of us have lost touch, but a re-union one day might not be entirely out of the question.

Our original goalkeeper was one of the youngest members of the squad. Jimmy Prickett, a strapping lad and another dedicated Mansfield fan, was a natural shot-stopper who also fancied himself as a centre forward. He is probably best remembered for having his brief 'international' career curtailed in the strangest of circumstances on a pre-season tour that I'll tell you about in the next chapter. A rival for the number one jersey was the team veteran Pete Spencer, a wiry bald thirty-something whose appearance belied some much-celebrated heroics between the sticks. Like my Dad, Pete was an ambulance driver who worked alongside him at King's Mill Ambulance Station on the outskirts of Mansfield. His claim to fame was keeping Oxford United goalkeeper Steve Hardwick out of the local Thoresby Colliery team in his youth.

A lynchpin of the defence was my great West Indian friend Andy Williams, whose 6ft 6ins frame towered above the rest of us. Dominant in the air, he could also retrieve the ball in any given situation on the ground, courtesy of his spider-like legs. His appearance in those days bore resemblance to Nottingham Forest's great full back of the day, Viv Anderson. Andy's Dad Audley was the most enthusiastic supporter any team could wish for, and got so wrapped up in a game that he may as well have been wearing the strip. One bewildered referee received so much grief from him one eventful Sunday morning that he brandished a red card in his direction.

Beside Andy was red-haired trainee builder Kevin Price, who was uncompromising in a tackle and, despite his unhealthy craving for cigarettes even at that early age, became a key member of the squad. In fact, he was responsible for one of the most important goals in the club's short history. Our midfield was graced by the artistry of 16-year-old Billy Land, a natural footballer if ever I saw one, with great vision and the sweetest right foot. Whilst he was the playmaker, Brian Sharratt was the general. Brian was an academic who excelled in every subject through regular school and sixth form, and unlike your typical swot was a true star on the football field. A great help in getting our club established, he played for Leeds University upon leaving school to pursue his education but rarely missed a Sunday morning.

Up front, we relied on the goalscoring prowess of pocket rocket striker Ian Hawkins, a young miner who was a real poacher inside the 18-yard box. His pace was the perfect foil for goalscoring partner Tony Brazier, who, at the age of 21, was one of the senior members of our team. Tony wasn't in our circle originally, but integrated quickly to become a real talisman. Another senior player was left winger Chris Leonard, the brother-in-law of defender Kev Price, who reminded me so much of that great Stags winger of the Seventies, Jimmy McCaffrey. Give the moustached juggler an inch of space on the touchline, and off he would go, weaving his magic before delivering an endless supply of assists from the left touchline.

I captained and – along with my Dad – picked the team, and spent my Sunday mornings filling the gaps between central defence and the left side of midfield. The goal-hungry left boot of my junior school days had long-deserted me. Now standing over 6ft 2ins, I was more comfortable at the heart of the defence, or adding my industry to the talents of our midfield. Though no star, I was passionate and committed, and a good organiser, if I say so myself. Needless to say, I assumed the role of team captain with a great degree of pride.

Our first season in a rough, uncompromising men's league as mainly 16 and 17-year-olds was a tough baptism, but one we came through with a great deal of credit. Playing on the open expanses of the Carrs, which presented a challenge for any footballer on a windy day, we won more than we lost, but learned some pretty severe lessons in on-field combat from some hardened encounters with tough-tackling veterans from local footballing and mining strongholds like Blidworth and Shirebrook. Our first competitive fixture was a local derby. Weeks before the game, the banter and needle began to escalate as we prepared to take on Warsop based pub team the Hare & Hounds. Despite the rivalry, there was an underlying mutual respect within both camps. Though we lacked in experience and physical strength, we did have an edge in terms of technical ability and managed to get off to a storming start to our league campaign with a satisfying 3-1 victory, detailed in the notes I kept at the time. The bragging rights belonged to us, but there was a re-match to follow later in the season, of course …

Imagine how confident we had become after going unbeaten in our first five games – a run that came to an end in the kind of agonising circumstances that only the great game of football can inflict. We had come from behind against Kirkby-in-Ashfield factory team J. W. Smalley, thanks to Leonard's 87th minute equaliser. But a last-gasp goal left us on the wrong end of a 4-3 scoreline. Our next game, against a poor side called Charcon Tunnels, also ended in defeat, but this overly-eager team captain must take some of the responsibility. Allowing my youthful exuberance to get the better of me, I was out of bed at the crack of dawn to shovel snow off the pitch in the hope that the referee would deem it playable. The prospect of a Sunday morning void was just too much to bear, but the prevailing conditions became a true leveller and three late goals left us nursing the wounds of a 6-3 defeat.

That first season continued to teach us some rather harsh lessons that, in time, we would benefit from. League leaders Shirebrook BRSA were an uncompromising, physical outfit whose superior strength helped them to wipe out our two-goal lead with a late flourish. We had been beaten 4-2. If that experience could be described as physical, our away game against Shirebrook's championship rivals Blidworth was positively brutal. This battle-hardened unit intimidated us from the first whistle. Hawkins was pole-axed by a challenge that Dad thought, with all his First Aid experience, might require an ambulance. It was the least enjoyable 90 minutes of football I had ever endured, and the 6-0 scoreline seemed a small price to pay for walking off the park in one piece.

Tough experiences in the sporting arena can make you stronger, but can just as easily destroy you. Thankfully for us it was the former, and a gritty 1-1 draw away to Shirebrook was a mark of our progress. Trailing with just 20 minutes remaining, we continued to dig deep and it was my flick on from a free kick that Hawkins blasted into the back of the net to clinch a well-deserved point. That return fixture against rivals Hare & Hounds was looming, but revenge was sweet as they coped much better with the muddy conditions to thump us 4-1. Nevertheless, our heads didn't drop and we all felt we had a point to prove when Blidworth arrived at our Carrs ground for the final game of the season. Unbeaten and cruising to the title, our visitors must have been expecting an easy morning against the boys who whimpered to that defeat a few months earlier.

How wrong they were. Six months in a no-holds-barred men's league had seen us come of age, and we very nearly emerged with a creditable draw. Leonard had cancelled out Blidworth's early breakthrough and a 1-1 scoreline was on the cards when a deflected shot just four minutes from the end sentenced us to a cruel defeat. Call it character-building if you like, but those early Mansfield & District Sunday League encounters couldn't have prepared us better for our second season, when we achieved the unthinkable. We actually won the league! The young guns of Warsop Rangers were Division 10 champions, but not before we had tasted success of a different kind – in Europe!

CHAPTER 6

FROM WARSOP TO EUROPE

Warsop Rangers Football Club's relentless sale of scratch cards - a popular means of fundraising in those days - funded the majority of a club trip to Belgium in the pre-season of 1982, where we played two matches during a six-day tour. It was an amazing experience, with coach, train and ferry journeys and a hotel stay all for the princely sum of £25 a head! If you've ever been on a club tour abroad, be it football, cricket or rugby, you will no doubt appreciate my recollections - even though they may have become somewhat embellished by the vast quantities of two-pint Belgian steins we consumed as part of our big match preparations - and celebrations.

From our hotel base in Ostend, we travelled by coach to our first game in the beautiful city of Bruges. Our opponents, Sint Joris, had a stadium that many senior non-league clubs would die for. The team coach, the stands - and a considerable crowd - made us feel like professionals, and we really were living the dream. In Belgium, all the sports clubs apparently received considerable government funding to develop modern facilities that benefited the entire community. Joris had several teams, from senior to junior level. Our facilities on the night were a far cry from the cramped, damp council Portakabins we were used to getting changed in on a Sunday morning back home.

Our plans did suffer an unexpected blow soon after kick-off, however, when goalkeeper-turned-full-back Jimmy Prickett was stricken with stomach cramps. Could it have been pre-match nerves, we wondered? Nothing of the sort! It turned out he had devoured a generous bag of plums earlier in the afternoon, and could not prise himself away from the toilet for long enough to return to the pitch. Despite having to re-shuffle our ranks, those of us who had the distinction of pulling on the second generation golden jerseys (and the new Warsop Rangers warm-up tops we had especially for the tour) couldn't have been more motivated. As captain, it was my duty to exchange a carefully home-made pennant with my opposite number, and at the shrill blow of the referee's whistle, our first taste of European football was underway. The pace of our opponents' passing game really took us by surprise. For the first quarter of an hour or so, their red shirts swarmed all over us. So different was their style of play, they told us in the club house afterwards that they considered us physical. In truth, we weren't in the same league in the kicking department as some of the Sunday sides we clashed with back home, but we gradually adapted to the tempo and stamped our presence on the game.

Our goalkeeper Pete Spencer - the senior member of the team - became the hero of the hour, saving a first half penalty before goals by Ian Hawkins and Chris Leonard clinched a 2-1 victory. According to the locals we were the only visiting foreign team ever to beat Sint Joris, which was a rather large feather in our respective caps. The game wasn't without its casualties, though. I aggravated a foot injury but worse still was the sickness our defender Glenn Hobson suffered when he met a powerful headed clearance on top of his head, rather than on his forehead. It ruled him out of starting the second game, but also that evening's long celebrations. Glenn, introduced to us via one of my Dad's work colleagues - was a classy defender who had played at a good level for Clipstone Miners' Welfare youth team alongside that future international Gordon Cowans.

Goalie Pete was the life and soul of any party, so it was no surprise when he stole the show in the Ostend bar that became our local. With hindsight, a group of raucous English youths suddenly spilling through the door on the first night must have appeared rather intimidating to the regulars, who were a little reluctant to welcome us with open arms. In fact, when one prickly Belgian poured a pint of beer into Pete's shirt pocket the tension in the bar cranked up a few notches. There was an uncomfortable silence. Then Pete, in his own inimitable style, laughed off the incident in such a way that within minutes, the perpetrator was buying the next round of nectar-like Jupiler lager. But Pete wasn't finished. Away from the football pitch and the blues and twos, he was a talented organist and positively lit up when he spotted a Yamaha, or something similar, in the corner of the bar. Before you could say 'Chas And Dave', Pete had ousted the resident musician and was rattling through a rendition of some good old favourites.

In another bar, one of our squad members had paid the price for scoring what he thought was a memorable brace. It didn't take the smooth talking striker long to attract the attentions of two glamorous girls, strategically perched high up on bar stools. He must have thought his prospects were akin to a penalty kick until the duo suddenly diverted their flirtations to another unsuspecting reveller, leaving our man with a hefty bar bill. The girls' commission must have been healthy that night, as we had to have a whip-round to finance the rest of his trip. Meanwhile, a few more rather naive team members beat a hasty retreat after making themselves comfortable in what turned out to be a busy gay bar full of moustached canoodlers.

Unfortunately, our prospects of a second foreign scalp were severely jeopardised by some poor planning by the tour operator. Strangely, we were not informed in advance that we would be making the long journey to Boom, near Antwerp on the Dutch border for our second match only 24 hours after our opening game – a strange turn of events considering we were out there for almost a week. Even a day's rest in between games would have given us the chance to recharge our batteries. Much of the time in between had been spent celebrating, of course, and an impromptu game on Ostend beach on our first evening in Belgium had gone on far longer than ideal, given our unbridled enthusiasm. So, as you can imagine, we were more than a little leg weary by the time our coach rolled into our next destination, a modern football and athletics stadium with posters hailing the arrival in town of 'Warsop Rangers – England' as SC Vitesse's next opponents.

This team was younger and even better organised than the Bruges outfit, and moved the ball around too sharply for our leaden limbs to chase in searing heat. Even though I missed a near post header that I should have buried early in the game, and had a low shot well saved, we were distinctly second best and probably did well to contain it to a 4-1 defeat – Tony Brazier bursting through the middle to shoot past the 'keeper for our consolation. However, we did claim one English victory that evening, when our left-back Gary Cooke flexed his biceps to win an arm wrestling match against one of the locals. The trip was a great success and the stories and exploits of that week have been inflated to legendary status over a pint or two in the years that have followed. The success of the tour set us up perfectly for our championship-winning season, but the league campaign began without me. A stubbed toe, aggravated in the Saint Joris game, had resulted in an impacted joint that would keep me out of action until the following February. I don't mind admitting I was a poor spectator.

CHAPTER 7

CHAMPIONS

A year older, and a good deal wiser, the young guns of Warsop Rangers began the 1983-4 campaign full of confidence, hope and expectation. That fantastic experience in Belgium was the perfect pre-season tonic, so when our Division 10 season kicked off in early September there could be only one result. Charcon Tunnels, the team that had beaten us 6-3 on that snow-bound pitch little more than six months earlier, were our unfortunate visitors and were sent back to the pub for a lunchtime beer on the wrong end of a 13-0 defeat. Mansfield Colliery were beaten 6-1 a week later, before Westfield Wanderers conceded 11, including Tony Brazier's third hat-trick in a fortnight. Rangers were rampaging and went on to win our first seven games, including a 2-0 away victory at Selston – a result that would prove priceless come the end of the season.

The first team to deny us both points (it was two points for a win back then) was another of those teak-tough teams from Shirebrook in late November. We drew 1-1 at home, and were held to the same scoreline on their patch early in the new year. Shirebrook, managed by an enthusiastic local sportsman Ian Wales, had title aspirations of their own, and despite our remarkable unbeaten run of 16 games, silverware was far from assured. Selston, a well organised team of veterans with the stature of prop forwards, were contenders, too, while Dale Sports were also within striking distance. Tension was embedding itself deep within our ranks when Kev Price earned us a share of the points with Selston, and a single-goal verdict over Dale Sports.

There was no margin for error as the season entered its final five games, but suddenly we were in danger of blowing it. Charcon Tunnels, the team we had hit for a baker's dozen on the opening day of the season, made us scrap for a 3-2 win and Dale Sports really put the proverbial cat among the pigeons by beating us 2-1. Playing without the confidence and fluency that had served us so well all season, our title hopes suffered another dent when mid-table Bowl FC held us to a 1-1 draw with just three games remaining. Then, as it turned out, anything less than a victory at Rufford Colliery on the penultimate weekend of the season (April Fools' Day, incidentally) would have cost us the title without question. And it was very nearly a 2-2 draw. With seconds remaining, a corner proved to be our final roll of the dice. Central defender Price, who had already popped up to score a couple of vital goals, powered forward and, to our absolute delight, piled in a last-gasp winner to keep the dream alive.

Despite losing only one game, we had surrendered top spot to Selston, who had forged two points ahead of us with only one game to go. We simply had to beat Central FC at home and hope that Selston would be beaten at Shirebrook. A point there would have been enough for them to steal the glory, but our local rivals – resigned to finishing third at best – were the best possible opponents we could have wished for, and certainly had a point to prove.

Ruled out through injury, I took the nerve-wracking decision to drive over to Shirebrook just a few miles away to watch the game that our title hopes depended on. Joining me on the touchline was our leading scorer Tony Brazier, sidelined by a neck injury and a worrying loss to our faltering ranks. Back then, there were no mobile phones, so it was impossible to relay the scores back to our home ground. The tension was unbearable, but Shirebrook eased our anxiety by scoring not once, but twice – and without reply. At the final whistle, we leapt up and down on the spot in celebration – much to the consternation of Wales, who was vociferously bemoaning his team's own failure to win the league themselves.

Selston had been beaten, and had finished on 34 points. Victory three miles away for Rangers would put us, too, on 34 points, but would secure us the title by virtue of a superior goals tally. That short drive seemed to last an eternity, and I could barely lift my head to gauge the reaction of our own team and supporters who were waiting in a huddle by the changing rooms to discover their fate. Had we managed to beat Central? Or had they deprived us of the win we so desperately needed? Had Shirebrook done us the favour of all favours and beaten Selston? Or had the team threatening to pip us at the post carved out the result they needed? The possibilities were endless, and chewing over the connotations was mind numbing for us all. As I turned my car into the entrance to our home ground, I began to flash my headlights in an attempt to convey our good news as quickly as I possibly could. And without an inkling of our result, Tony and I instantly knew we had achieved the unthinkable when about 40 arms were flung aloft at the sight of my illuminating lamps. Rangers had beaten Central 4-1 and we were champions indeed – thanks only to a superior 13-goal margin.

Tony, despite missing the final game, had scored 30 goals in as many games – a fine strike rate for a striker at any level – while winger Chris Leonard had contributed a remarkable 21 in 22 games. Their performances epitomised everything we had strived for, and walking up to lift the cup at the annual presentation dinner at the now defunct Devonshire Suite at Sutton-in-Ashfield a few weeks later was akin on our scale to taking those hallowed 39 steps at the old Wembley Stadium. Warsop Rangers lifted the roof off the popular venue that night, long before the demolition men moved in, and celebrated all over again when former Stags winger Russ Allen presented the trophies at our club presentation evening.

Ours had become a remarkable journey, and every member of the club played their part. But despite my own vision and determination at the outset, we wouldn't have achieved what we did without my Dad's tireless commitment behind the scenes. His knowledge and devotion quickly established him as a role model for the boys and each of them fully appreciated his input. He became the definitive club secretary, keeping the paperwork up to date and even marking out the pitch with sawdust on a Sunday morning. In those days, we hadn't progressed on to lime. So imagine his dismay then when one half-baked referee reported him for failing to provide clearly visible goal lines. It turned out that a bunch of kids had got to the goalmouth before we kicked off one Sunday morning. Back at League headquarters, where Dad had earned the respect of Ken Burgess and his committee, common sense prevailed, and Dad was quickly exonerated without a blemish to his record.

Digression: It was at the Devonshire Suite that I met the late, great George Best in the early Eighties. He was the celebrity speaker as a sportsmen's dinner, and I had been sent along as a fledgling cub reporter to interview the footballing legend for the Chad. It was probably the worst interview I have ever conducted. Star-struck, and still rather shy at that age, I remember being stumped for any kind of worthwhile reply when he volunteered to tell me all about the Antabuse implant he had just had to deter him from drinking any more alcohol.

CHAPTER 8

IT NEVER RAINES BUT IT POURS

The following season, 1984-85, we were elevated from Division 10 to Division Seven in one leap and, with a similar squad, maintained our progress. One notable addition to the squad was a young Kevin Gee, who went on to manage local senior non-league side Glapwell before taking over the hot seat at Rainworth Miners' Welfare, these days of the Northern Premier League. Another string of comfortable victories followed, and with them a glut of goals. But two teams had our clear measure and both did the double over us as we settled for a creditable fourth spot.

Football, like most sports, is a great leveller and the worst performance in our short history came at the worst possible time. A home game against eventual champions Ashfields co-incided with the unveiling of our new team strip - green and yellow stripes with black sports - and the new sponsor who had provided it was on the touchline watching. Ashfields, spearheaded by the renowned footballing family the Fisher brothers, overwhelmed us and a string of brilliant goals earned them a rather humiliating 10-1 verdict. Despite their brilliance, we buckled tamely and deserved the good hiding we were given.

On Ashfield's heels was another young team from Mansfield Woodhouse, who played under the name of Sherwood Colts. Their charistmatic manager Eric Neville had some talented players, many of whom went on to play at a higher level on a Saturday afternoon. 'Nev' was well known on the local curcuit and his son Dean was a useful player who established himself in the Sutton Town squad.

Inevitably, the core of the original Warsop Rangers team began to diminish the following year as life took certain players in different directions, and the adventure for me reached a natural end. But soon after my Dad and I put together another successful Sunday League side, Valentino's, with the help of my cousin Mark Taylor – a staunch Stags fan and a keen Sunday morning player himself. We were sponsored by the new nightclub that had opened in Mansfield at the time, Valentino's – a regular haunt on Friday and Saturday nights, some time after the legendary town centre hot spot Digby's had closed its doors for the final time.

As well as securing a sponsor, I also persuaded former Mansfield goalkeeper Rod Arnold to come on board as coach for a spell. It was a strong line up, so it wasn't surprising that we clinched success in both league and cup. Some of the original Warsop Rangers players joined us, including Andy Williams and Tony Brazier, who became lynchpins of this club, too. Tony crashed home a remarkable 49 goals in 33 appearances in all competitions (missing only one game).

However, one player, in particular, shone in the new red shirts. Clint Guy had been a young professional with Mansfield Town in the early-Eighties but was now spearheading the attack for 1982 FA Vase finalists Rainworth Welfare on a Saturday afternoon, as well as gracing us with his presence the following morning. Such was his talent that I could never understand why he hadn't been given the opportunity to ply his trade at Field Mill instead of performing magic tricks with a football just for fun. Clint really was a magician with a football and regularly scored the type of goals that left you open mouthed in admiration. Thumbing through the old record books I discovered that Clint scored 41 goals in 26 games in our first season, becoming our leading marksman in the league with 30 – one ahead of his potent partner Brazier. With such a lethal strikeforce, we won the Division VII championship, reached the quarter-final of the County Cup and the final of our league's junior cup, only to lose 2-0 in a replay against Ravenshead Sherwood Rangers.

It was as captain of Valentino's that I crossed swords with one of Clint's Rainworth team mates, the late Alan Raine, who had been a key member of that club's amazing Vase story. Alan, who was BBC Radio Nottingham's man of the match at Wembley, was turning out for Bilsthorpe Celtic in the Mansfield Sunday League, and I was about to pit my wits against the Wembley hero. Bilsthorpe were a good side, as you would expect, and whilst we were a capable outfit, too, we were still finding our feet at this higher level. A draw, then, away from home, was our main objective. My task was to stick to Raine like superglue, and mark him out of the game, and for 89 minutes our masterplan remained intact. The match was petering out with the score at 1-1. I can't remember who drew first blood, but I followed Raine everywhere, harrying, menacing and stifling the genius that could have torn us apart at the flick of a cultured left foot. I was focused and determined, driven on by the fear that if I dropped my guard for a second, we could be punished and our hard graft would be rendered worthless. I knew time was ebbing away, and we deserved our point. Then disaster struck.

A long searching pass from another Bilsthorpe player aimed to pick out the surging forwards, but our well marshalled defence was quick to advance and the off-side snare was about to prompt a waving flag. Confident enough to leave Raine in the trap alongside them, I, too, advanced towards the half-way line. But our own centre forward, back helping his defence, lost his concentration, and left them all on-side. The flag stayed down and an incisive pass found Raine's grafetful feet. In a flash, he had dispatched a precision shot from the edge of the box past the helpless dive of our goalkeeper Kev Newton (later to become secretary of another decent local senior club, Teversal). It was 2-1.

With only seconds remaining, the referee re-started the game, but Raine remained motionless in the centre circle. I glanced round instinctively to gauge his where-abouts, and there he was, not two metres away from me, with satisfied hands on resting hips. "Stay here, Simon. I'm not going anywhere now," he quipped. The final whistle blew, and Raine had won them the game. I had come agonisingly close to completing what would have been a notable personal achievement, but had been denied not by my own failing, but by a team mate's momentary lapse. It was a stark lesson to us all that players of Raine's calibre can turn a game in the blink of an eye. Alan sadly died following an illness while still in his forties.

Through my twenties, I played Sunday football for several other clubs, including Bilsthorpe Welfare and Sutton-in-Ashfield based Traveller's Rest – a talented young team from a pub run by ex-Mansfield Town skipper Sandy Pate. In fact, it was for Traveller's that I scored perhaps my best ever goal in men's football. I'll refrain from slipping back into Roy of the Rovers mode here, but I must say that it was a rather spectacular scissor kick from just outside the six-yard box that ended up in the left-hand corner of the net. For someone who wasn't renowned for his goalscoring prowess, it was a pretty special moment.

In total, I must have played in about 250 Sunday League games over a 10-year period and emerged relatively unscathed, knees and other joints intact and richer for some wonderful memories of playing competitive football at grass roots level for some very well run clubs. From a personal perspective, none of them could ever match the journey and camaraderie that made Warsop Rangers so special, from its unlikely beginnings to its European adventure and its crowning glory, our league championship.

Digression: As I approached my late twenties, my footballing career was beginning to grind to a natural halt. Though at this stage engrossed in the game on a professional level, I began to dedicate my leisure time to that other passion of mine, the horse. For the first time since my early teens, I was back in the saddle and looking forward to riding competitively on my newly purchased steed. The foundations of another exciting career were taking shape.

CHAPTER 9

FOLLOWING RAINWORTH TO WEMBLEY

I've enjoyed some amazing afternoons on the terraces as a football fan, particularly during those passion-charged teen years when Saturday afternoons were considered wasted if there wasn't a live match to be watched - usually at Field Mill, and occasionally at Forest's City Ground or even Chesterfield's previous home Saltergate. But following Rainworth Miners' Welfare to Wembley in 1982 was something quite magical. You know, when you witness something unfolding that you instantly acknowledge may never happen again in your lifetime.

Non-league football in North Nottinghamshire in the early Eighties was in a pretty healthy state, and along with 12,000 others, I made the pilgrimage to Wembley to support Rainworth in their fairytale Vase Final against Forest Green Rovers, just a couple of months before I got my lucky break as a trainee journalist. To an impressionable, football mad teenager, the players the late Brian Phillips assembled became overnight heroes. I recall standing at the top of Wembley Way, soaking up the atmosphere as the Rainworth team coach crawled between those of us who were paying homage to the stars who lived, worked and played among us all. Through the windows I could pick out defender Trevor Sterland's rugged grin, and the beaming face of midfield terrier Brian Knowles. Waving along with them was semi-final goal hero Dave Hallam and winger Paul Comerford, moulded in the style of Forest's great Scottish international John Robertson. I could also see Alan Raine, too. They must have been completely overwhelmed. I know I was.

On the day, Rainworth's trusted battle plan that had seen them triumph in eight previous rounds was readily penetrated by an upwardly mobile Forest Green side who, in truth, were technically superior. Simple as that. Following the 3-0 defeat, some questioned Phillips' decision to stick with his tried and tested formation, which may have left them tactically vulnerable. Yet in my view, adopting a new unfamiliar system would have represented an even bigger gamble, and may not have prevented defeat anyway.

To my mind, the achievement of Phillips and his squad - the whole fantastic journey - completely overshadowed the result. Rainworth had become the first miners' welfare team and only the second truly amateur squad to play beneath the hallowed twin towers. Their players still paid weekly subscriptions! The fact that so many local people followed them to Wembley is testament to the magnitude of their achievement, which has rightly become etched in local footballing folklore. Perhaps it should have been the very foundation for a fast track through the non-league pyramid, but in those days ambition didn't stretch beyond subsequent Vase quests, and further domination of the Notts Alliance. That said, it's pleasing these days to see the club performing with enough ambition to have scaled the non-league pyramid to a level that no other miners' welfare club has ever reached.

Looking back, the semi-final second leg victory over Barton Rovers at Rainworth's tiny Kirklington Road ground conjures as many vivid memories as the day out at Wembley itself. The first encounter in deepest Bedfordshire had ended in a goalless draw and the sheer emotion generated by 5,071 local people - a Vase record outside of the final to this day - was uplifting, the anticipation quite overwhelming. There were no stands or turnstiles at the Kirklington Road ground. No terrace steps either. Just a rope to cordon off the playing area where the white shirts of Rainworth would do battle with their Southern League rivals. The sheer emotion generated by a partisan crowd, crammed around a touchline that had only ever been trodden by bucket and sponge-carrying local league managers and the inevitable man with his dog, was uplifting.

It was as if fate had decreed that Rainworth could not possibly fail in their quest for the highly improbable. This was a real-life football fairy story, and Wembley was their destiny. So there I was, balancing on a milk crate by the corner flag as powerhouse centre forward Hallam – a local policeman - crashed home the winner 12 minutes from time. Rainworth won it 2-1, and uproar ensued. A young presenter by the name of Nick Owen – later of 'GMTV' fame – was dispatched to provide a match report and interviews. Suddenly, my first ever visit to football's mecca beckoned.

In seasons to come, I got to know manager Phillips personally through following his team's fortunes for the Chad. I always respected his quiet, steely approach and was impressed by the respect he commanded in his dressing room. As a player himself, Phillips - a centre-half with Mansfield Town - had served a jail sentence for his part in the bribery scandal that plummeted football into disrepute in the Sixties. But his remarkable achievement at Rainworth that year certainly diluted any stigma his dubious past may have burdened him with. While Phillips the motivator organised his team on the pitch, club secretary Alan Wright organised the club off it. Wright's contribution to that golden era in Rainworth's proud history cannot be over-stated, so how fitting it is that since his death in 2002 the wrought iron gates at the club entrance honour his achievements in the style of a lasting tribute to another great man, Bill Shankly. Sadly, Phillips is no longer with us, either, having passed away in the spring of 2012.

The chance of watching live football with my mates at any level was always irresistible but the entertainment on the terraces was much better than the action on the pitch at Chesterfield one winter afternoon in the Eighties (the norm at Saltergate in those days, I hear you snigger). Intent on finding a game to watch somewhere in the snowbound area – my mates and I ended up over the Derbyshire border for the Spireites' encounter with high-flying Huddersfield Town, managed by Mick Buxton. There had been heavy snow fall and the pitch had to be cleared before the game could go ahead, but what happened next would never be permitted in the modern age. A full scale snowball fight broke out between the Town fans and the home supporters on adjoining terraces. As we were among the home fans down near the corner flag, we duly joined in the fun. Imagine the scene as dozens of snowballs rained down amid riotous laughter, with the policemen guarding the perimeter fence grinning their approval.

Another amusing day on the terraces was at Forest back in the Eighties when the great Brian Clough marched onto the field of play to apprehend a supporter who was rampaging around the centre circle dressed as a clown. Some of you will recall the outrageous fan, who must have been expecting to be dragged back to the touchline at any moment after pulling off such a stunt, but not by Cloughie himself. I enjoyed a bird's eye view of the whole incident from the Trent End and applauded with approval of such an unlikely custodian, along with thousands of adoring Forest fans.

I was no stranger to the terraces on the other side of the Trent in those days. My uncle John, who still lives in Nottingham, was a devout Notts County supporter so many of our family visits conveniently co-incided with a home game at Meadow Lane. That's where I first met the late, great Jimmy Sirrell, a good friend of my uncle and without doubt the most colourful manager in the club's long history. Sirrell would be among the guests at family parties at the Lane and although he probably wasn't too fond of idle football chatter with this eager young man, I certainly appreciated the spellbinding football he served up during County's surge to the old First Division in 1981. Ian McCulloch, Trevor Christie and Rachid Harkouk were at the sharp end of many County victories. In fact, it was McCulloch who spoilt the party when Notts upset League Champions Aston Villa on the opening day of the 1981-2 season.

My thirst for watching football also led me back to Central Avenue on several occasions, where Worksop Town were doing battle in the old Northern Premier League. It was a good standard of football – just about equal to the Conference of the more modern era – with good teams like Runcorn, Altrincham, Marine and Matlock Town regularly on the Tigers' team sheet. Central Avenue was the member of an exclusive club, as, like Northampton Town's County Ground, it was also the home of cricket and for that reason had only three terraced sides. Beyond the far touchline was the immaculately maintained square where Nottinghamshire would play host to those County Championship rivals once every summer. It was also the scene of what was to become my finest moment with a cricket bat, when I shared in that century opening stand against Worksop's boys. In fact, I was turning out for Welbeck's firsts at Central Avenue when news came through that Notts County had pulled off that shock result at Villa Park. Today, of course, that charming old ground is no more, as the Tigers play at purpose-built stadium across the town.

I had cherished my formative years on the terraces, especially at Field Mill, but by the age of 17 was beginning to wish they would soon be coming to an end, because now I had an ambition to realise. I remember ambling out of the West Stand following Mansfield's 1-0 FA Cup defeat by Doncaster Rovers (a look back through the record books tells me it was November 1981), and glancing up from the gloom at the illuminated press box from where radio reports were being broadcast live, and up-to-the-minute copy was being strung to the nationals. I so much wanted to be a part of that, and promised myself that one day soon, I would be up there. Fate deemed that I would be, and perhaps much sooner than I thought.

CHAPTER 10

HOLD THE BACK PAGE!

At careers conventions in the school hall, I adamantly declared ambitions of becoming a sports reporter. But one career's officer told me, in no uncertain terms, to let go of such a fanciful idea. I was a working class lad in a mining village and a perfectly respectable job down one of the local pits was a much more sensible objective, he reasoned. The thought of scaling a dark mineshaft filled me with dread. My Dad had worked in the mines, as an electrician, and many of my mates headed underground at the age of 16. I had nothing but admiration for the men - and boys - who crawled along the coal face, but it wasn't for me. I had my dream, and though the odds were probably against me (just as they had been when I dreamed up the idea of forming my own football club), I wasn't about to let them go in a puff of coal dust.

As my second year in sixth form at the Meden School began to draw to a close, I wrote speculatively - by hand, not on my typewriter - to my local newspaper, the Chad, enquiring if they had any vacancies for trainee reporters. There was no advertisement in the 'sits vac' column, but I thought it worth a try, as I had no desire to do anything else. An uncle who held a responsible position with the National Coal Board (the NCB) suggested that I might be looked upon favourably for a draughtsman's apprenticeship, while another recommended following his footsteps into the police force. Then there was graphic design. I enjoyed art, and was studying for an A Level, so art college might have been a more appealing alternative.

To my surprise, I received a swift reply from editor Jeremy Plews, announcing that he had not one, but two vacancies, for junior reporters. Was this fate, I wondered, or would my hopes come crashing down as quickly as they had been suddenly built up? My first interview went as well as could be expected, and he seemed impressed by my clutch of neatly typed match reports and a self-designed Warsop Rangers handbook. I left, somewhat disheartened, however, when he told me he was seeing about a dozen graduates all eager to apply their university degrees to a career in journalism. Perhaps it was his way of letting me down gently, I thought.

Imagine my delight, then, when I got invited back for a second interview, just before my 18th birthday. I'd passed my test, and drove to Mansfield in my Dad's red Talbot Horizon to learn my fate. "You must know that I haven't asked you to come back here for nothing," exclaimed the editor, and at that moment I knew I was about to be given the opportunity of a lifetime. A week the following Monday,

I would turn up to work as a trainee reporter at the Chad, suited and booted and flushed with shyness. I don't know what Jeremy saw in me that he didn't see in the other interviewees, but he gave me a chance I was determined to grasp with both hands, and to this day I remain eternally grateful.

Something the paper's managing director Nick Linney said to me when he welcomed me to the company has stuck with me ever since. He reasoned that what made journalism such a wonderful career choice was the fact that it could, eventually, give a trainee like me the key to pursue my passions in life, whilst getting paid for doing so. In other words, prove your worth, cut your teeth and you may get the opportunity to specialise in a subject you are passionate about. But before I could nurture any dreams about becoming a sports reporter I had to start at the bottom – the very bottom. That meant picking my way through an endless pile of obituary reports, fetching tea for the thirsty sub-editors and making frequent journeys to the local shops to buy sandwiches, chocolate bars and copies of the paper's main competitor, the Nottingham Evening Post.

However, it didn't take long for me to graduate onto proper news stories, under the watchful eye of news editor George Robinson, a fun-loving personality who brought me out of my shell in those formative months. Tragically, George died at a young age following a short illness a couple of years ago and I deeply regret that I didn't find out in time to pay my respects. Anyway, I'd be out in the villages interviewing disgruntled residents, filing copy about petty criminals from the town's magistrates court and rounding up the latest developments from the parish councils – arguably an even more boring job that typing up those deathly obituaries! I even succeeded George as the paper's pop columnist, which was a wonderful job for a music mad lad like me. Every week I would receive padded brown envelopes stuffed with all the latest releases to review, and free concert tickets fuelled my interest in all kinds of live music.

In between two stints at college to complete my journalistic qualifications, I was beginning to sink my teeth into more beefy issues. There was a story about neglect at a local hospital, under the banner headline 'BARBARISM ALLEGED' and my first photo by-line. I was first on the scene when Robin Hood's reputed hide-out the Major Oak in the heart of Sherwood Forest caught fire. Some of the Crown Court reporting was mesmerising, in particular a manslaughter case involving characters from my home village, but nothing touched me more than the months I spent reporting on the Miners' Strike of 1984. As a young man who had grown up in a mining village, my coverage of endless protests, rallies and picket lines was decidedly poignant. Many of the faces I wrote about were familiar ones. Friends who worked at Warsop Main on the fringes of the Derbyshire coalfield and Welbeck Colliery in the stronghold of Nottinghamshire were directly affected by the upheaval, and some were at loggerheads.

Many of the men I played football against on Sunday mornings were mineworkers – several were team mates - and the occasional encounter between my own team Warsop Rangers and opposition from over the Derbyshire border brought divided opinion into stark focus. Times were tough, as we were reminded when we turned up for one Sunday morning game in Ashfield fully expecting it to be called off due to heavy snow. It was so deep the ball wouldn't roll without turning into a giant snowball, but the referee was a striking miner who wasn't going to forego his £7 match fee. The game is on, he insisted, but it became the most outrageous match I ever took part in. Fortunately for us, we won 8-2.

Despite blossoming into a fully fledged news reporter, writing about sport remained my burning ambition and Stan Searl, the legendary sports editor at the time, probably got sick and tired of me tapping on his office door and asking if he would like yet another cup of tea. I would be itching to talk football with the great man, and find out a little bit more about his work, so it wasn't long before opportunities began to present themselves. Stan began to hand me 'fag packet' reports from local league secretaries to type up for that week's paper, and I was in my element.

CHAPTER 11

LEARNING FROM A LEGEND

Stan Searl was an institution in local sport, and I admired and respected him even before I started working in the same office. His were the match reports I eagerly thumbed through as a schoolboy when the Chad dropped onto the doormat on a Wednesday morning. He also reported on the Stags for BBC Radio Nottingham, covering close on 1,000 games for the station. He was, quite simply, Mr Mansfield Town. Stan had spent much of his working life in the local hosiery industry, entering into journalism by sheer chance well into his forties. He had a passion for amateur sport, particularly football, and was secretary of his beloved Skegby Welfare in his younger years. Because of that involvement at grass roots level, he pieced together his sports pages with the same dedication as those who religiously provided him with their club's weekend scores every Monday morning.

Never reluctant to peer above his horn-rimmed glasses and give me the benefit of his experience, Stan began to shape me into the sports journalist I have become today. In fact, there's no doubt his advice became the cornerstone of everything I have gone on to achieve in football, and latterly in horse racing. The single most important lesson he taught me was to develop a strong working relationship with the characters I was writing about week in, week out. His own relationship with directors, managers and players was built on trust. Earn that, and they will confide in you, he told me. Invariably, you will get the story before your rivals. Betray that trust, and you will be the last to know ...

Stan was right. Such was his standing at the football club in his heyday that the Field Mill board and management always tried to release their big news stories to him first. Usually, it would be on Chad deadline day (Tuesday) so that Stan could get the exclusive scoop in the next morning's paper. I remember Stan reflecting fondly on the close friendship he forged with Stags boss Dave Smith during his tenure in the Seventies, and how Smithy would regularly pop round for a cup of tea with him and his devoted wife of over 60 years, Dot.

Fundamentally I aspired to be like Stan. Not just because I wanted to scoop the opposition and be the best, but because I wanted to earn the same professional respect that managers and players - household names - had for him. Over the years, developing strong working relationships with football managers and players - trainers and jockeys - and winning that professional respect has quite frankly meant even more to me than the opinions readers and listeners have held about my articles and broadcasts. Experience of working in that environment also gave me a full appreciation of the life of a professional footballer, the way a Football

League club operated and how games were approached and played. Stan also had exacting standards, from the way he conducted himself around the football club and in the community; the accuracy of his writing and in his own appearance. Imagine then, his distaste when I turned up to accompany him on the team bus to Port Vale – without a tie! With a pointed finger, and within deliberate earshot of the directors, he told me in no uncertain terms how he expected me to dress the next time. Embarrassed though I was, another lesson had been learned.

Soon I became a regular in the Field Mill press box, giving up my Saturday afternoons to sit beside Stan and observe. The press box was a buzz of activity, and I learned quickly how to read a game, and interpret the action accurately and succinctly. At that time Stan was one of three doyens of the local sporting media to cover The Stags. There was Albert Stapleton (father of the Nottingham Evening Post's former Notts County correspondent David), who would string copy to the Saturday paper, the Football Post; and Jack Peat, who covered home games for the Sunday nationals amongst others. Stan combined the role of radio reporter with that of Chad scribe, and also found the time to string out a bit of lineage himself.

Thirsty for knowledge, I even spent one afternoon crouched beside the North Stand goal with the Chad's best sports photographer Roger Grayson, clicking my way through a reel of black and white film. It was all great experience, but nothing to compare with the lessons gleaned from my first ever live broadcast in 1985. The Stags were playing Exeter City at Field Mill, and BBC Radio Devon, for whatever reason, couldn't send a reporter on the long journey north. Stan, unable to fit the coverage into his busy schedule, decided to throw the young boy into the fray, and though wracked with nerves, I wasn't about to decline the opportunity. The sports producer arranged to cross live to me for a 30-second report roughly every 15 minutes. I would also be required to give a half-time and full-time resume. So, after the opening exchanges, I carefully scripted a few paragraphs on my notepad and read them back quietly to make sure my reports were the correct length. In those days most communications were by telephone. We didn't always have use of a lip mic or the benefit of better quality ISDN connections. Stomach churning like a tumble dryer, and palms dripping, I sat ready, poised for the phone to ring.

When it did, the studio presenter gave me my cue and the line to Field Mill was live. At that second, my heart missed a beat. A goal was scored, and the notes I had been carefully scripting had been rendered useless at the sudden kick of a ball. Flummoxed, I began to ramble with heavy breath, trying my best to describe the goal without the benefit of a prompt. As I garbled the scoreline and handed back, I tried to regain my composure before beginning to script my second report, due midway through the half. I painstakingly repeated the process, but imagine my horror when seconds before my next live piece, another goal hit the back of the net. For the second time, my notes were suddenly worthless, and off I ventured into another frenzied burble of mumbo-jumbo. This was already a baptism of fire when, for good measure, fate ensured that the third and final goal of the game again went in just as I was about to deliver another live report. A few days later, my Dad bumped into a friend in the village who had been holidaying in Devon and had heard my report on the radio. "He made it sound very exciting," he said, politely.

Aside from football, Stan built up extensive coverage of the thriving local cricket scene, introducing the weekly 'Star Match': a league game that one of us would cover in person, along with a photographer. Afterwards, we would present a medal to the winning team. Stan was also responsible for the success of the cricket scoreboard. To get your name in this, you had to take at least one wicket and score a minimum of 10 runs. It was essential reading, and from club to club, a performance good enough to get your name in print became widely knows as a 'Chadder'. Stan was also widely respected among the extensive local bowls community and along with dozens of local players made the pilgrimage to Skegness every summer for the national championships – a highlight in his work calendar. He was a keen golfer but loved his job equally, so it was no surprise that he agreed to stay on and impart his vast knowledge in a part-time capacity to first Tim Morriss and them myself in our roles as sports editor at the paper. It was great to have him around during my first years in the hot seat, advising on how to deal with potentially difficult situations that would arise from time to time at Field Mill.

Stan passed away in 2002, aged 82. Born in Huthwaite in Nottinghamshire, he had served in the RAF during the Second World War and began a 20-year career in the local hosiery trade after being demobbed in 1946. He joined the Chad as a reporter in 1966, and covered his first Stags match three years later – a 2-1 victory over Reading. He later became the author of 'Mansfield Town – A Complete Record 1910-1990' which quickly sold out. I'm delighted to say that I have a signed copy of this collector's item that has been an invaluable resource in researching this book. Fittingly, Stan sat beside me in the press box when the newly rebuilt Field Mill was officially opened in August 2000. As Chad's current sports editor John Lomas fondly recalled in a tribute: "It was lovely to see Stan come back for that game as if he had never been away. I think Simon had problems getting the microphone back off him that afternoon. Stan was really in his element."

Jeremy Plews, editor of the Chad at the time, acknowledged the "enormous debt" the paper owed him. "He transformed the paper's coverage of the local sport scene through hard work, enthusiasm and unrivalled knowledge of his subject. He gave every sport the same consideration, whether professional at Field Mill, bowls or pub darts." Those sentiments were echoed by his great friend Joe Eaton, the long-serving Mansfield Town secretary who sat on a similar pedestal during his distinguished career. "He was not only a reporter but also a true friend and supporter of the club. Stan did a lot of good things behind the scenes for Mansfield Town," he said. All three tributes encapsulate what was so special about him. Another glowing accolade was the surprise 'This Is Your Life' style evening that was put on for Stan at the Mansfield Civic Centre upon his official retirement as sports editor. All the good and great of the local sporting scene took to the stage to share stories and memories before BBC television's polished sports presenter Andy Knowles handed over a red book full of messages. It was moving to be there.

Digression: Stan's close friend and long-serving club secretary Joe Eaton was also a great help to me right up to his untimely retirement. In fact, the board of directors in those days were men of great integrity who were all incredibly accessible. John Pratt, the chairman and owner of the club's parent company Abacus Lighting, and his right-hand man Geoff Hall were only too happy to offer frank, honest statements about the club's off-field activities. Directors John Almond and John Brown were successful businessmen in their own right who were always engaging. Indeed, the respect they always showed Stan (and his young apprentice) was always re-assuring.

Joe was the first face I usually saw on my regular journeys to the football club and it was always a pleasure to spend half an hour chatting with him about the club's bygone days. The exploits of legendary striker Ken Wagstaff was his favourite topic, though like me, Joe was a racing man who enjoyed talking horses. On reflection, I don't think I ever met anyone in the game who commanded as much respect as Joe. Club secretaries from far and wide would ring him for advice, and no manager enjoyed doing business with him over an impending transfer more than the late, great Brian Clough. When retirement was forced upon him on the arrival of new chairman Keith Haslam in 1993, Joe was the longest serving club secretary in the Football League, having started in 1956 after an injury brought a premature end to his playing career. Quite aptly, Stan dubbed him 'Mr Mansfield Town' and it was my honour to help him organise a well-deserved testimonial match against Forest that Clough himself attended.

CHAPTER 12

THIRD DEGREE BURNS

As I came to the end of my teenage years, I was resigned to being a Sunday morning footballer, as Saturdays were spent honing my skills as a young sports reporter with the Chad, covering the local non-league scene as well as helping out in the Field Mill press box. But I do recall many a happy hour at Sutton Town's old headquarters at Lowmoor Road as a player, as well as a scribe. My claim to fame in those days was signing Northern Counties League forms with The Snipes as a back up, though in truth they would have been faced with the injury epidemic of all time to consider calling me up. I did turn out for the reserves on occasions, however, and trained with the whole squad up at Lowmoor on cold midweek evenings. Though I enjoyed the work-outs, these sessions enabled me to build a stronger rapport with the players and coaching staff I was writing about week in, week out.

Steve Giles, a good friend of mine who these days shares my passion for owning racehorses, was one of several club managers I worked with at the time, and enlisted the help of the great Kenny Burns to coach - and coax - his squad in their quest for success. Burnsie was, quite simply, a footballing great. Transformed by Clough to become Footballer of the Year in his heyday, this Scottish international and king pin of Forest's glory days in Europe was giving a bunch of willing amateurs the benefit of his vast experience. It was at one frosty training session that Kenny's bellowing Scottish brogue bit me as hard as any of his trademark tackles.

During a small-sided game, I angled a searching pass with my favoured left foot, aiming to pick out a team mate in the opposite corner of the pitch. It was actually a decent pass that did reach its destination, and for a split-second I was rather proud of it. Unfortunately for me, Burnsie wasn't. "Hey, yeeuu, Glenn Hawdle," he growled in his unmistakable tones, whistling play to a halt before lecturing me on the virtues of the short game. I wasn't sure whether I wanted the pitch to swallow me up, or whether I should offer some kind of mitigation. Afterall, I was only the local reporter enjoying a kick-about, and surely didn't deserve the coach's wrath. But in Burnsie's eyes, I was as much a player as the rest of his squad during that session, and I'd just ruined the flow.

I looked forward to pulling on the claret jersey for an occasional run out in the Snipes reserves, and after getting acquainted with just about every park Portakabin in the district on Sunday mornings, it was a real privilege to play at a proper ground like Grantham Town's, for example. And for a true amateur parks player like me it was exciting to play alongside the likes of former Northampton star Gary Saxby in a Snipes friendly at Aston, near Worksop. However, it was an evening fixture against Belper Town at Lowmoor Road that had me questioning whether it was about time I put away the boots and spent more time wielding the pen. Early in the game, a stray elbow made contact with my brow and bloodied my shirt, before a donkey-style kick from a flat-footed defender sent a searing pain down my right shin. Always one to see the humorous side, colourful club chairman Steve Cook quipped afterwards: "Look at Simon. He doesn't know which one hurts him the most." An hour or so later and I was sat in the casualty department of the local hospital, having my facial wound butterfly clipped and my leg X-rayed for a suspected fracture. Examinations revealed only heavy bruising, but it was enough to bring my season to a premature end.

Despite his odd sense of humour, I had the greatest admiration for the chairman and what he set out to achieve. Steve, owner of the local Hardwick Motor Company, poured his hard-earned cash and his valuable time into the club during the mid-Eighties when, with Bryan Chambers at the helm, he built a team good enough to move up the pyramid of non-league football. He wore his heart on his sleeve and his spats with referees and linesmen were often more entertaining than the matches themselves. At their expensive peak, The Snipes boasted some of the best non-league talent in the Midlands. Paul Millns, another excellent sporting product of Clipstone village, was a commanding figure at the back; Andy Kirk brought flair and creativity to the midfield; and Martin Coupe and Mark Richardson were regular goalscorers in the Northern Counties League. Manager Chambers, a likeable Geordie, was rewarded for his success with The Snipes when he secured a move to Conference club Stafford Rangers. It was a big job for Bryan who gave me the opportunity to break the story.

During that period, the senior non-league scene around North Nottinghamshire was buoyant and I thoroughly enjoyed reporting on it. Some of Sutton's pre-season friendlies I covered for the local paper in those days gave a sparse handful of diehard local football followers an early glimpse of some of the game's finest talent. I recall a young Irish boy called (Roy) Keane, who had been added to a very young Forest squad one July afternoon. A gangly black teenager called (Carlton) Palmer whose elastic legs pulled together a fledgling West Brom side. And a young man by the name of (Clayton) Blackmore who wore the Manchester United jersey with eye-catching distinction. However, those who turned up to watch Central Midlands League club Oakham United take on Brian Clough's Forest in a pre-season fixture were denied the chance of seeing striking starlet Nigel Jemson in action, after he apparently ended up at the wrong Oakham. Instead of reporting for action at the old Mansfield Hosiery Mills ground (now a B&Q), word had it that he found himself driving aimlessly around the picturesque Leicestershire town of the same name.

Rainworth Welfare, still revered for that Wembley appearance a few years earlier, continued to command their share of column inches in the local press and I followed them on many a Vase adventure to northern outposts such at St Helen's Town and Guiseley. Meanwhile, quality players ensured that Huthwaite added strength and depth to each season's Notts FA Senior Cup. The two clubs met in a well attended final at Eastwood Town's ground in 1987, won by Trev Wass's Huthwaite. It was an exciting game to cover, with such strong players as Colin Thacker, Paul 'Taxi' Marsh, Andrew Ferenc, Kieren Smith and Richard Denby in their ranks. Huthwaite had as strong a team as any in their pomp, but without the necessary foundations the club sadly disbanded. Smith and Denby moved on to Gresley Rovers and played in an FA Vase final for the Staffordshire club. The former was an exciting player who was always a threat in front of goal – perceptive and clinical when he had to be. Denby, by contrast, was a true architect who would never wear out a pair of boots but could thread the ball through the eye of a needle to pick out a telling pass.

Looking back, it is sad that Sutton Town were unable to survive a difficult decade without losing their identity. Sad, too, that Oakham United disappeared without a trace under that enormous DIY centre. The Hosiery Mills ground that was their home was one of the finest sports grounds in the area. And sad that Huthwaite were unable to capitalise on their success at a time when they had a team good enough to compete at a higher level. Despite the array of talent on the field of play, the underbelly of the non-league scene in the north of the county back then was stilted by the same financial constraints that football clubs at a similar level are faced with today.

CHAPTER 13

DEBUT AT THE OLD SHOWGROUND

My Mansfield Town 'debut' for the Chad came in August 1984, when I was dispatched to The Old Showground to cover the club's League Cup first round tie against Scunthorpe United. Stan was on his annual sojourn to Skegness to cover the bowls championships among a fraternity who respected him just as much as their footballing counterparts. I had gained vital experience covering the local non-league scene, but now my name really would be in lights. I recall to this day my nervousness as I climbed onto the team coach in the West Stand carpark. Quietly, I slid into my seat a few rows from the front and sat as quietly and inconspicuously as I could, in complete awe of the familiar faces around me. Kevin Hitchcock, Colin Calderwood, Tony Lowery, Noel Luke, Dave Caldwell ... I could hear their banter and spirits were high. Two rows in front of me were the directors, who were joined a few moments later by the great man himself. Silver hair gleaming in the sunshine, his sheer presence overpowering the space around him, the manager Ian Greaves took his seat, and we were off.

It was that trip when Ian suddenly rose from his seat and sat beside me. He always had time for me, which I appreciated, and although my shyness and youthfulness left me completely in awe of him in those days, he did make me feel at ease whenever I was in the club's inner sanctum. He didn't speak more than a few sentences on this occasion, but what he did say before patrolling further down the aisle stuck with me. "If there's anything you want to know, or anything you need, come to me son," he said. This great man-manager instantly put me at ease, and made me feel an acknowledged member of the team party. Suddenly, I had the confidence to sit straighter in my seat, drop my shoulders and enjoy my first team 'debut'.

Apart from penning my first back page report, I was particularly looking forward to the match for another reason. Neil Pointon, whom I knew from school, was in the Scunthorpe team and I was determined to have a chat with him before the game. Neil, or 'Wimp' as he was known to his mates, was a year below me at the Meden Comp, but was already making the most of his apprenticeship with The Iron. I'm not at all sure to this day why he had such a nickname, as he certainly wasn't a wimp in the true sense of the word. It was about an hour before kick-off, and I was standing in the tunnel waiting for the team sheets. Sure enough, Wimp was playing at left back, and peering through the door marked 'Home Team', I could see his curly locks amid the claret and blue shirts that hung from their pegs in readiness for combat. As we made eye-contact, I forgot myself for a few moments, and found myself inside their dressing room and deep in conversation with the kid from Warsop Vale. It must have been the sudden change of expression on Wimp's face that made me aware that our discussion wasn't entirely going un-noticed. As the young left-back slumped back onto the bench with a blush, I turned to see the Scunthorpe manager Frank Barlow scowling at me from a pace away. He didn't say much. Didn't need to. I mumbled a hurried explanation and made myself scarce, amid the chuckles of the United team. Barlow shook his head with a gaze of disbelief. Time to take my seat in the press box, I thought.

Over the years, I followed Neil's career with great interest, penning many a feature on his progress in the Chad. I sat for hours with his late father Wilf, who travelled the length and breadth of the country watching his son in action. By the time Mick Vinter had secured The Stags a 1-0 win at the Old Showground that evening, Wimp was already attracting the attention of First Division scouts. It was no surprise then, when he was prised from the Fourth Division strugglers by Howard Kendall's Everton after four years and 159 first team appearances. The Champions splashed out £75,000 to sign him - a significant cash injection for a basement league club in those days - and pitched him straight in at the deep end. Neil went on to establish himself as a first team regular at Goodison Park, winning a Championship medal of his own before eventually rejoining Kendall at Manchester City for the princely sum of £300,000.

More top flight action with Joe Royle's Oldham Athletic followed, and I can remember catapulting myself off the sofa when he scored the opening goal in the 1994 FA Cup semi-final against Manchester United at Wembley. Unfortunately, Mark Hughes bagged a last-gasp equaliser and you might recall how United went on to crush Wimp and his team mates in the replay. It was a thrill to have gone through school with a future First Division football star, and it was always a pleasure to catch up with Neil on some of his visits back home. For the record, he went on to play for Hearts in Scotland before having spells with Chesterfield, Walsall and Hednesford Town. Last I heard he was working for Bolton Wanderers' Academy as a coach, but he's one of those old friends that you inevitably lose touch with.

My match report at Scunthorpe made it into print, but I don't recall covering another Stags first team game until exactly a year later. A surprise 2-0 victory over Middlesbrough at Field Mill in August 1985 had given them a great chance of progressing to the second round of the League Cup, and drawing one of the big clubs. Naturally, I was hoping to accompany Stan to Ayresome Park for the Tuesday night tie but got much more than I bargained for when he summoned me into his office the previous day. Stan was staying back to work up to deadline, and was relying on me to file the match report in time for Wednesday morning's paper. I was oozing with pride. Stan clearly trusted me to deliver the goods. I've arrived, I thought to myself in a rare moment of private smugness. However, I was blissfully unaware that Stan had a back-up plan, just in case his apprentice messed up. He had decided to write his own match report from the BBC Radio Nottingham broadcasts that were being provided throughout the evening by another stand-in.

So there I was, sitting beside Newcastle United's all-time great Jackie Milburn (who was working for the local media) in the Ayresome Park press box, poised to scribble the observations that would be read by 35,000 Chad regulars by daybreak. It was a thriller, and the words flowed from my pen in a torrent. The Stags had drawn 4-4 with goals by Micky Graham, Neville Chamberlain, Mick Vinter and Mark Kearney, and were on their way to Stamford Bridge for a mouth watering second round tie against Chelsea. Excited by the result, and convinced that Stan would approve of my efforts, I made my way back to the team coach, looking forward to reading my report on the back page at first light. Fortunately for me, Stan was so impressed with my work that he committed it to print in preference to his own fail-safe version. I must admit I was a little deflated when he admitted with a chuckle the next day: "I was going to write it myself you know, but yours was better." I think they call it a back-handed compliment, and a compliment it was, I reasoned, once I'd thought it through. We'll talk some more about that game later.

Something else happened that night that amuses me to this day. Like me, my Dad was an avid Stags fan and had made the journey to the North East in a minibus with my cousin Mark (of Valentino's FC) and a handful of other dedicated supporters. Half-way up the A1, a punctured tyre caused them to miss the kick-off, but their spirits were buoyed by a rip-roaring performance. Not one to crave the limelight, Dad struck into song, and couldn't believe his ears when, to the tune of 'She'll Be Coming Round the Mountain ...', several hundred Stags fans echoed his words. "We've been driving up the A1 on three wheels - on three wheels ..."

During those formative years as a football reporter, I enjoyed following the fortunes of the young Stags in the FA Youth Cup. Managed by John Jarman, whose enthusiasm for the game knew no boundaries, they set off on a giant-killing cup run in 1984, reaching the quarter-final. It was an exciting night at Vicarage Road when the Stags met Elton John's Watford starlets, who proved just too good on the night. The following season Jarman's juniors were at it again, this time knocking Manchester United out at Old Trafford - another game I was proud to report on. It was my first visit to the Theatre Of Dreams. United fielded a strong side including young Sutton-in-Ashfield midfielder Wayne Bullimore, who was just a few years in front of their famous 'Class of 92' (Beckham, Giggs, Scholes, the Nevilles ...). The blond starlet had been tipped for great things but never actually made a first team start for the club. He later moved on to Barnsley and had spells with Scunthorpe, Peterborough, Scarborough and Barrow.

Jarman's crop of aspiring professionals provided the first team with some serious home-gown talent. Craig McKernon was later sold to Arsenal for £250,000, while Simon Coleman went on to play at the highest level with Middlesbrough and

Looking the part in that first Stags kit, circa 1970.

In the saddle on my third pony Hoppy, circa 1975.

The all-conquering Welbeck Colliery youth team of 1981. I'm standing second right. Holding the trophies is captain Neil French. Kevin Gee, better known as manager of Glapwell and Rainworth football clubs, is the tiny boy to my right.

The first Warsop Rangers line-up, 1981.

Champions! Proudly showing off the Mansfield Sunday League Division XI Trophy.
My Dad Dennis is far left.

A job well done. Dad and I at our Warsop Rangers presentation do.

Check out those haircuts! Meeting new Stags signing
Charlie Bell at a Field Mill open day in 1981.

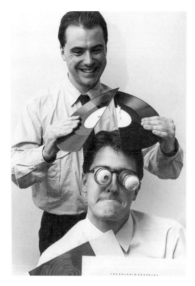

Celebrating our victory in Europe. Spot me buried under Brian Sharratt's armpit. Goalkeeper Pete Spencer, back left, raises another Belgian stein before rattling off a few more tunes on the organ.

Having a smashing time as the Chad's pop columnist, circa 1983.

Englishmen abroad … Warsop Rangers line up for our second game in Belgium, 1982.

Above: Top team.
Valentino's FC.
Coach Rod Arnold
is back row, fourth
right, and Clint Guy
is back row,
far right.

Right: Gimme the ball!
In action for
Sunday League club
Valentino's FC.

Left: The fledgling
broadcaster.

Below: Award winners!
Forest reporter Andrew
James, left, and BBC
Radio Nottingham's
sports producer Martin
Fisher join me in
showing off our radio
awards.

Arseing about! Stags' clown
prince Phil Stant.

The Radio Nottingham Sports Team circa 1998,
from the left: Robin Chipperfield, Colin Slater,
Alex Trelinski, me, John McGovern and Colin
Fray.

Nostalgic! Back at Field Mill for the 'Meatpies &
Microphones' photo shoot.

Taking the Mac!
Sharing a joke with
racing pundit John
McCririck on Sky
Sports' At The Races,
2007.

Exclusive interview ... with top Irish jockey Joseph O'Brien at Doncaster on Sky Sports'
At The Races, 2012.

Bolton Wanderers. Les Robinson and Ian Stringfellow were others whose stars were in the ascendancy. Robinson had spells with Stockport County, Doncaster and Oxford United before returning to Field Mill as skipper later in his career. Stringfellow became a Wembley winner in 1987, though never truly fulfilled his potential to play at a higher level. Other Stags coaches deserved plenty of credit for honing future talent. Ivan Hollett, a goalscorer for Chesterfield in the Sixties, was a stalwart behind the scenes while scout and former mineworker Bob Shaw worked closely on the youth policy before eventually moving on to scout for managers at a string of top clubs.

CHAPTER 14

AROUND THE GROUNDS

Though Stan Searl was on the verge of retirement, it was still something of a surprise when Jeremy Nicholas, the sports editor at BBC Radio Nottingham at the time, rang me out of the blue to offer me the job as the station's Mansfield Town reporter for the new 1989-90 season. Jeremy, who went on to present Channel 5's football coverage before returning to the East Midlands, wanted me on the team for Mansfield's first League game away to Chester. Stan, now helping me in my role as Chad sports editor – a position I had been awarded the previous year - was closing in on his 1,000th broadcast and was rightly disappointed not to be given the chance to reach that landmark. I understood his feelings, but this was an opportunity that I didn't intend to ponder and he was nothing but supportive.

Saturday 19th August was a memorable day for several reasons. George Foster, who had taken over from Ian Greaves earlier in the year, was about to begin his first full season as manager. It was also Chester's final season at Sealand Road, and the last time the Stags would play there before it became a retail park. It was also my debut for Radio Nottingham and I had travelled up on the team coach, where the importance of a good start had set a tense mood. The Stags had struggled the previous season and had added only David Hunt from Notts County and former Chesterfield defender Steve Prindiville to the squad.

Nerves danced in the pit of my stomach on the build up to 2pm, the time when the station's Saturday afternoon sports show got underway. Once Jeremy and Martin Fisher had set the scene for the Forest game and Colin Slater had revealed Notts County's line up in his big match preview, it would be off to the new boy Simon Mapletoft at Sealand Road. My notes were carefully prepared, and I must confess that in those formative days, I still wrote myself a script whenever possible.

Perched at the press bench in shirt sleeves on a hot, sticky afternoon, I prepared to deliver my opening burst down a designated BBC telephone line and, though no doubt a little rushed, it came across relatively flawlessly. The nerves began to settle, but only ever so slightly, until my attention was grabbed by the reporter sitting to my left. It was none other than cricketing ace Mike Hendrick, the former Nottinghamshire, Derbyshire and England seamer who was about to try his hand at a spot of radio reporting before venturing back into cricket as coach at Trent Bridge.

Though I admit to feeling a little overawed by the occasion, Mike appeared completely overcome by it, and could barely compose himself as he prepared for his opening cue from the Radio Trent studio. Fumbling with his notes, his unsteady hand – the same hand that had perpetrated 87 Test wickets – failed to prevent a plastic cup of piping hot tea from spilling onto his trousers. Mike mumbled something about his spilt tea live on air and I felt genuinely sorry for him, but at the same time drew a certain confidence from seeing such an iconic figure struggling beyond his own comfort zone. Mike went on to become an accomplished after dinner speaker.

Laila Bishay, the technical wizard who was driving the programme behind the scenes, settled me into the role with some lighthearted chit-chat and her lovely calm tone helped me get to 5.30pm with my reputation intact. I don't remember much more about the occasion, but the Stags got their season off to a flying start with a 2-0 win, thanks to goals by Trevor Christie and Steve Charles. Predictably, the players' mood was much more relaxed on the journey home, and I shared their enthusiasm. My radio career was up and running.

Chester eventually went on to play their home games at Macclesfield Town's Moss Rose during the construction of their new stadium, and the cramped press facilities at what was then a non-league ground made match reporting rather challenging. Back in the early Nineties, we were still broadcasting down telephone lines, and the big cream front-dial phone provided to me by the local BBC station had to be balanced on my knee as there was nowhere else to put it. In a scenario that would have modern day health and safety inspectors doing hand stands, the long cable to my phone was plugged into a landline socket several yards away. The cable sat menacingly across a row of wooden terracing, masquerading as a trip wire, and surely enough, the second one poor unsuspecting spectator got his boot underneath it the handset went flying off my knee and into the crowd.

Health and safety were two words at the forefront of my mind whenever the Stags were scheduled to meet Swansea City at the old Vetch Field. It was a fixture I loathed with a passion. Firstly, the long meandering five-hour journey through the depressing industrial backdrop of Port Talbot into deepest South Wales was mind numbing, to say the least. But it was the fate lying ahead of me when I reached the Vetch that really filled me with trepidation. The majority of the press and media reporting on the Swans did so from a relatively comfortable press box high up in the main stand behind the dugouts. But the BBC reporters met with an altogether different fate. The BBC gantry sat on scaffold high in the roof of the opposite stand. It consisted of a wooden bench on a platform accessed only via a metal ladder that must have been at least 30 feet high. Halfway up, the ladder appeared to swing from its hinges, leaving this reporter clinging on with white knuckles.

I've never been fond of heights, so scaling the ladder was an ordeal I had to steel myself for a good few days in advance. The gantry was so high up that bags and equipment had to be winched up by ropes separately. And if climbing up wasn't bad enough, then crawling back down was equally un-nerving. The workspace was dotted with the deposits of visiting pigeons and large enough only to accommodate the BBC Wales reporter and his visiting colleague. The adjacent view of Swansea Prison did little to lift the spirits, though I did crack a smile on one visit when the Stags supporters behind the goal to my right sang in unison "Simon, Simon give us a wave." I did, to the strains of a sympathetic cheer.

Despite the rather daunting facilities, there was always a warm enough welcome at the Vetch, but by contrast, one trip to Ninian Park proved intimidating. The Stags were taking on Cardiff City and fellow Stags reporter John Lomas and I were entering the main stand to make our way to the press box when we were apprehended by a rather terse policeman. Despite the fact that we had little more than telephones and notepads in our possession, the unfriendly officer treated us with an unexpected suspicion and a total lack of professional respect and insisted that he searched our baggage. The incident infuriated John who took it upon himself to write a letter of complaint to the Chief Constable in South Wales, though I'm not sure he ever received a reply.

I first met John at an away match at Huddersfield Town on Grand National day, 1989. I was reporting for the Chad and Radio Nottingham, whilst he had been assigned by the Nottingham Evening Post as their new Stags reporter, taking over from Nick Lucy. John soon earned enough credibility to secure a seat on the team coach and we became travelling companions for the next 13 years. You couldn't wish to meet a more affable, sincere fellow and I held him in the highest regard as a journalist and a friend. John was passionate about football and had a real zest for life. Speedway in his home town of Long Eaton was another passion, along with an unquenchable appetite for gigging in and around Nottingham in pursuit of bands I had seldom heard of. He also had a curious interest in the macabre and would amuse us on long away trips with the contents of some dubious magazines. But he also had an uncanny knack for getting into bother in often amusing circumstances, as you will discover.

Reporting at Fulham's Craven Cottage presented problems of a different kind for both of us. At the Cottage in those days the pitch was completely out of sight for much of the game. That's because the phones were housed beneath stairs underneath the press box. Dialling up to fire over a quick radio report, or string over a few paragraphs of copy, couldn't be done without the risk of missing developments up on the pitch. Of course, we didn't have the luxury of mobile phones in those days.

Preston North End's Deepdale stadium was another test for the visiting man from the BBC. Curiously, the radio points were housed in what can only be described as a two-man pigeon loft above the tunnel, accessed by another ladder. Once up there it was cosy, to say the least, as there was just enough room to share with a rather rotund reporter from BBC Radio Lancashire who was particularly fond of the custard slices that were handed up to us during every game. It was during a visit to Deepdale that John attracted the unwanted attention of a group of Preston fans who were blocking his view from the main press box. Despite asking them as politely as possible to remain seated, they persisted and soon began snarling abuse through the window. After the game, and thinking no more of the disturbance, John made his way out of the ground and back to the team coach, only to be spotted by the youths and chased down an alleyway parallel to the ground. In evading his pursuers, the unfortunate reporter snagged his brand new leather jacket on a barbed wire fence and looked rather disheveled when he eventually staggered up the coach steps a few moments later. Needless to say, our travelling party wasn't as sympathetic as we should have been on hearing John's breathless though descriptive explanation of his close encounter.

It was at another Lancashire venue that I delivered a line that had the entire Wigan Athletic press box erupting in laughter, and the laughter was very much at my expense. The big story leading up to the match at Springfield Park was the news broken to me at the club's pre-match gathering at a nearby hotel that Scottish right-back Malcolm Murray had failed a fitness test. He had tweaked a groin and would not be in the starting line up. In my haste to reveal my scoop, I informed my dedicated listeners – and my colleagues from the media – that "Murray is out after pulling a groin overnight". I'm certain Malcolm did nothing more than enjoy a good night's sleep, but my Freudian slip inferred something far more spicey.

The depressing atmosphere that envelopes a stadium when a club is down in the doldrums can, as a visiting reporter, crawl under your skin. The tension in the corridors leading to the dressing rooms, as well as up on the terraces, contaminates the air all around you. God knows I've experienced it at Field Mill often enough over the years. But never have I been so moved and affected than on my visit to a doomed Aldershot towards the end of the 1991-2 season. The club was, quite literally, on its knees, and was about to go out of business. The Stags, by contrast, were gunning for promotion and had no trouble winning a game that, days later, would be struck from the record books. Managing The Shots at the time was former Mansfield player Ian McDonald, who had picked up the poison chalice when former Ipswich Town and Arsenal star Brian Talbot resigned earlier in the season.

McDonald earned my greatest admiration that evening for holding together a post-match press conference in the most challenging of circumstances. The result was of no consequence. Here was a man who was powerless to prevent imminent bankruptcy from closing down a Football League club and, taking with it his job and the livelihood of his players and staff. It was a hollow victory indeed for The Stags, and a sobering reminder of the fragile state of football finances in the lower divisions at the time. 'Mac' stuck by his stricken club until the axe finally fell on 25th March 1992 but deservedly made a quick return to the game as reserve team coach at Millwall later that summer. It was fitting, too, that he was invited back for a testimonial game when a new Aldershot rose from the ashes some years later.

Food at football grounds was a regular topic of conversation between John and myself. Another privilege of travelling with the team was tucking into a hearty pre-match meal at a nearby hotel on most away trips. Just as well, as the hospitality at some clubs was non-existent. The warmest welcome invariably came from the northern clubs, particularly those in Lancashire and across the Pennines in Yorkshire. Burnley's vast press room was among the best, serving up a buffet style mini banquet. Neighbours Bury offered a tasty line in meat pasties. But over in Rotherham, the pies were a definite highlight. Being in the same division as The Millers was a great antedote to those long trips to Swansea. The hot pies would be handed around the press box at half time, and I would sit happily upon an old bus seat on the front row munching through the golden pastry and sinking my teeth into succulent chunks of lean steak. I'm not sure if the Millmoor pies ever won any awards, but such accolades do exist to encourage better catering at football stadia. In more recent times, Morecambe have earned a reputation for theirs - another feather in the flat cap of the Lancashire football community.

Digression: A perk of the job as a football reporter was the privilege of rubbing shoulders with some of the game's true greats. Sitting beside the late Jackie Milburn at Ayresome Park in those formative days was awe-inspiring, and who would have thought I would be commentating beside Jimmy Armfield all those years after watching his Leeds United on that wonderful Elland Road pilgrimage as a boy. At Highbury one evening, I found myself in the company of another late great before a Nottingham Forest game I was reporting on for Radio Nottingham: England's World Cup winning captain Sir Bobby Moore, who was summarising for Capital FM. On visits to Preston, it was always humbling to be greeted by the club's ambassador and goalscoring colossus Tom Finney., while another legend, Nat Lofthouse, was always accommodating in his capacity as president at Bolton Wanderers' Burnden Park.

Few of the old time greats measured up to the pre-War superstar Tommy Lawton, whom I had the pleasure of meeting in the early Nineties. Tommy scored hundreds of goals for a string of clubs including Notts County, and was a columnist for the Nottingham Evening Post in his later years. He was living in a care home when I had the great fortune to interview him for Radio Nottingham. The minutes flew by as he reminisced. He recalled his career in remarkable detail, and I could have listened to him for hours. Tommy was a true gentleman and I consider myself fortunate to have held court with him on that magical morning.

Another proud moment came in the early Nineties when I met another of my broadcasting heroes, John Moston. I had joined the committee of the local branch of the Lord's Taverners, alongside my Radio Nottingham colleague Colin Slater, and enjoyed Motty's company at a function at Trent Bridge.

CHAPTER 15

LIFE ON THE ROAD

Over the years, I was fortunate to enjoy the privilege of travelling to hundreds of Mansfield Town away matches on the team coach, socialising with the players, staff and directors on long journeys and developing some firm friendships in the process. Being a member of the official team party also afforded me the chance to enjoy a pre-match meal with the players and staff. These days, I would expect to see pasta and fruit featuring heavily on the menu. Back then, our staple diet was gammon and chips – or a hearty all-day breakfast.

John Lomas, my constant travelling companion, ensured that most road trips were at the very least amusing – win, lose or draw. When John was around, there never was a dull moment. On one overnight trip to Exeter City, he ended up in some poor unsuspecting woman's front room when he mistook the steep staircase into her home for the entrance to the local pub! Several players had a penchant for a practical joke, and pulled off a perfect '10' performance to stitch up John and I on an overnight trip to Bournemouth in February 1993. We were sharing a room at the seafront hotel where the team was camped out in readiness for the following day's game. But it wasn't until after dinner, when we returned to our room, that we discovered that mystery pranksters had struck. The word 'Redrum', scrawled across the bathroom mirror in toothpaste, alerted us to the fact we had been invaded sometime between the steak and the coffee. For the movie buffs among you, it was a witty re-enactment of that famous scene from The Shining when Wendy sees the word 'murder' in the mirror scrawled backwards by her possessed young son Danny.

It probably came down to sheer luck on my part, but John came off much worse than I. Apart from rolling off my mattress with a clatter in the middle of the night to discover that a leg on my bed had been unscrewed, I did get off light. And as much as I sympathised with my ill-fated colleague, I found myself doubled up with laughter as the scale of the prank unfolded. His shirt sleeves were knotted, his socks snipped off at the toe. There was toothpaste in his shoes and shower gel in his bed. Word travelled swiftly along the corridor and although they never came clean, we had it on good authority that left back Chris Withe was the chief perpetrator, aided and abetted by striker Paul McLoughlin and that real dark horse, striker Steve Wilkinson.

It was on that same ill-fated trip to the south coast that I gained some revenge in the most poetic manner. At the turn of the year, upon joining the freelance ranks, I'd bought myself a state-of-the-art mobile phone in the hope that it would be useful in giving me that vital edge when it came to communication. Back then, hardly anyone owned a mobile, and those who did found them far too big to fit into any pocket. Mine wasn't exactly of building brick proportions, but was hefty by comparison to modern day cell phones, with a pull-out aerial to boost its signal.

Throughout the long journey south, I'd been ribbed mercilessly by assistant manager Bill Dearden and a number of the players for being just a little bit flash. But when the team coach developed an engine problem late on that Saturday night and juddered to a halt by the side of the M1 about an hour from home, the man with the mobile suddenly became the most popular member of the travelling party. The first to swallow a huge slice of humble pie and ask if he could make a quick call to the wife was Mr Dearden himself. Soon there was a queue for my Panasonic device, and at £1 a call the last laugh definitely belonged to me!

I should have been in for another windfall after winning the correct result competition on another away day. For a £1 entry fee, everyone on the coach was invited to forecast how the day's football fixtures would turn out – and the winner would scoop the proceeds. On this particular afternoon, I'd topped the table, but wasn't informed until after grinning competition adjudicator and treasurer Stuart Watkiss had spent my proceeds on a feast from McDonald's.

John and I almost never made it to a Brentford game when I agreed to drive defender Mark Smalley's car from Field Mill to the team hotel. In those days, players would often coax a non-playing volunteer into taking their car to the hotel or ground if they were intent on shooting off in that direction after the game. Having reluctantly volunteered, John agreed to come along for the ride but soon wished he hadn't. Thinking we would simply follow the coach all the way down the M1, neither John nor I felt it necessary to ask which hotel we were staying at – and where.

So imagine our reaction when Smalley's well-used jalopy began to lose power in the fast lane. As the speedometer dropped from about 70mph to 20mph, we were forced to pull onto the hard shoulder as the back end of the Redfern coach disappeared into the distance. Once the engine had cooled, its power returned, but we had lost contact with the team and were, we feared, stranded. There were no mobile phones in those days – Panasonic hadn't yet launched my hefty handset - so a quick phone call to ask for directions simply wasn't an option. The car continued to gain and lose power but we persevered on our long and fraught journey into the unknown. Fortunately, despite only a few crumbs of information and a bigger chunk of intuition, we eventually found our way to the team base in Watford, both vowing never to hop behind the wheel of a player's car ever again.

Journeys on the team coach always followed a familiar pattern. The manager at the time, together with his backroom staff, would occupy the front seats, along with the board of directors. Behind them, John and I would sit either side one of the few tables that separated the many rows of gaudy Draylon seats. Grabbing a table was always an advantage for writing up copy on my trusted typewriter – the same one my parents had bought me as a youngster. Towards the back of the bus the players would congregate. Some would sleep, others would listen to music and there was usually a highly charged card school in session.

Permission to travel with the team came with a few unwritten rules. It was frowned upon if a club tie was not knotted neatly around your neck. And late arrivals would pay a severe penalty. Players could expect to be fined, whilst John and I knew that driver Big Andy was instructed not to wait a minute beyond the designated time. As travelling guests, we were expected to be just as punctual on return journeys. Departure time on Saturdays was 5.30 prompt – unless the manager was indulging in another beer in his opposite number's office. The 'gaffer' was the only one allowed to stretch the rules. In midweek the coach would be pulling out of the car park no later than 10pm, so the pressure was always on to get the match copy phoned over and radio interviews wrapped up.

I'm happy to say that I was never late for the bus at Field Mill, and never got left behind on away days either, though demanding copy and broadcasting deadlines sometimes took the situation to the wire. Being the last one on board was a fate worse than death – particularly if the team had been on the wrong end of a dismal defeat. That said, I spent many an hour chatting to players and managers on those journeys to and fro, developing rapport and friendships to last. Stags midfielder Wayne Fairclough was once asked in an interview what he thought about the local reporters travelling on the team coach. It was a rare scenario, as the majority of football reporters across Britain had to make their own way around the country. Fairclough summed it up succinctly. "They're a part of the team. One of the lads," he replied. And we were.

Trips to Carlisle had a knack of proving eventful, as you will discover later, but on a bleak Saturday in November 2001 I chose not to travel on the team coach for a lunch time kick-off at Brunton Park and was left regretting my decision. The game was brought forward due to an England match and I was kindly offered a ride up to Cumbria by my friends from rival radio station Mansfield 103.2. The journey was largely uneventful until we were faced with a diversion due to a road closure somewhere in the frozen north. That was certainly inconvenient, but the thick fog and snow we encountered on the often treacherous A66 to Penrith was positively worrying. Suddenly the prospect of failing to make kick-off began to trouble me, as well as Radio Mansfield's commentary duo of Nigel Pinnick, who was driving, and a young Jason Harrison, who was making his first ever away trip. Only Steve Hartshorn, who ran the fanzine Follow The Yellow Brick Road, seemed unperturbed by the thought of becoming stranded, probably because of a giant-sized pack up he was munching through on the back seat. Had we been swept beneath a snow drift, the contents of that lunch box would have kept us all alive for at least a week!

The weather was closing in, but matters were about to get worse. Nigel had been quietly watching the needle on his fuel gauge disappear deep into the red and cautiously announced that if we didn't see a fuel station soon the car would almost certainly judder to an untimely halt. Fearing the worst, our driver gambled on taking a detour round local villages in the faint hope of seeing the bright neon-lit canopy of a filling station somewhere in the distance. By now I was convinced that Radio Nottingham would have to draft in a late replacement from somewhere. But eventually, our prayers were answered. The fuel tank was replenished and we made it to Carlisle just in time to report on a Stags victory, sealed by striker Chris Greenacre's 14th goal of the season.

CHAPTER 16

BUSKING IT!

The press box at Field Mill was always a hive of activity on a Saturday afternoon, but particularly hectic for me. It was not uncommon to be reporting on the match for Radio Nottingham and the local radio station following the away team. Sometimes it would be another BBC station, and on other days an independent. But the workload didn't stop there. Up to the end of 1992 I had the relative luxury of compiling my back page Chad report on a Monday morning in readiness for the Tuesday evening print deadline. But, upon leaving the paper and going freelance in January 1993, I was responsible for providing copy for the Nottingham Evening Post's renowned Saturday football paper, the Football Post, as well as the daily editions of the main paper.

In those days there was considerable interest in the lower leagues among the national press so I would always find the time to string together some snappy reports for a couple of Sunday papers, notably the Sunday People. Even when the game was over and the press box lights had been extinguished, my workload wasn't complete. Come Sunday morning I would be busy constructing what we call in the business a 'considered' match report for Monday's edition of the Evening Post.

However, one such report had to be pieced together in the early hours of a Sunday morning when my wife went into labour a week early. I had just covered the final match of the season, at home to Plymouth Argyle, and was relaxing at home with Jo when our second daughter Bethany began to give signs that she was ready to enter the world. Expecting a lengthy vigil at the local maternity ward, and worried about the possibility of missing my deadline, I fired up my computer on returning from a hasty hospital run and e-mailed Monday's article over to the sports desk. But for Bethany's eagerness, both our daughters would have conveniently arrived in the close-season. Our first born, Charlotte, was conceived at the very start of the 1995-96 season and was born three days late on 17th May. How's that for planning!

Anyway, Radio Nottingham's sports show always began at 2pm, so it was vital to be at the ground about an hour before 'air time' to plug in the telephones (or in later years of advancing technology the ISDN kit) and establish contact with the studio. My link there was the charming Laila, introduced in the previous chapter, whose job included cueing up all the reporters and recording the off-air highlights. Laila really was the lynchpin of the show but also worked as a news reporter on the station's John Simons' Show and on the production team of the television hit series 'Police 5', so certainly had a wealth of experience to call upon.

On the stroke of two, the opening music would fade into the self-assured voice of sports producer Martin Fisher, who succeeded Jeremy Nicholas and held the show together slickly from the York Street studios. First of all he would cross over to Nottingham Forest reporter Andrew James (and in later years Colin Fray) to preview the action at the City Ground. Minutes later, Colin Slater would be bellowing his thoughts on Notts County's prospects in his rich, unmistakable tones. Then, it was over to Simon Mapletoft at Field Mill. What were the Stags' prospects? How vital was it to secure all three points? Who were the opposition's danger men ..?

Once the scene had been set at our respective matches, it was time to go down to the dressing rooms and get the team sheets, which were always available 45 minutes before kick-off. Waiting for them in the tunnel area always escalated the excitement and tension of a game. Players and coaches would emerge from dressing rooms, taking with them a waft of linament every time the doors swung open. Some would exchange a few words with an ex-team mate before disappearing back through the door marked 'Home' or 'Away' to begin the big match build up in earnest. Then, I'd be back up to the press box to phone over the line-ups to the Post and stand by to deliver the breaking news across the airwaves in a concise 90 seconds. "George Foster has named an unchanged side as the Stags go in search of a vital victory ..." Interviews recorded at the Thursday morning press meetings would help to fill the next section of the build-up hour, before Martin swept around the grounds again for the final preview and confirmation of the line-ups. In what seemed like no time at all it was 3pm, and the game was underway.

Each half would be an endless stream of quick updates, roughly every 15 minutes, and goal news at it happened. Sometimes, on the bigger occasions, it would be a full commentary game – a blow for blow account punctuated by the incisive views of a guest summariser. In between all that I'd be dictating copy for the Football Post report that had to be phoned in to a copytaker in Nottingham. Laptops and wi-fi were still a thing of the future in the late Eighties and early Nineties. Notepads and phones were the universal method of recording and communicating news. By the final whistle, the press box was a buzz with breathless broadcasts and strained voices stringing over more copy to the nationals. "Let's go back to Simon at Field Mill where the final whistle has just been blown ..." In two or three minutes, I would have the afternoon's action wrapped up neatly into a final report.

The introduction to the Football Post's blow-for-blow account would be dispatched, and next the more concise resumés for the Sunday papers would be sent down to more fast-typing copytakers on another phone line. The Football Post was an institution in its heyday. It really was hot off the press and could be bought in town centre pubs and on street corners on Saturday nights, only a couple of hours after the final whistle. I remember dashing out for a copy as a kid, eager to read about that afternoon's action and see how my team fared in the back page league tables. Back then, the Football Post seemed to be at the cutting edge of quickfire news delivery. Apart from the classified round up on 'World Of Sport', 'Grandstand' or national radio, and a few choice reports on the bigger games, there was no other way of indulging in the detail of your local games.

At about 5.30pm, half an hour before the Radio Nottingham sports show turned into Dean Jackson's music programme, a considered breakdown of the latest epic would grace the airwaves, followed by the big match interview. On a victorious afternoon, there would be no shortage of volunteers. The striker who scored the winning goal, the satisfied manager … But if the points had been squandered it could be a tedious cross-examination of a dejected general who had just been let down by his toothless troops.

Now despite my ability to multi-task, I couldn't possibly have done all this single-handedly. That's why I enlisted the help of a young apprentice. There was never a shortage of teenage wannabes just itching to gain some hands-on journalistic experience at a live match. Over the years, I'm proud to say I honed the skills of several budding reporters, who all went on to enjoy a good career in their chosen field. Mark Hall, my first assistant and a trainee at the Chad at the time, became a fully fledged reporter at the paper; student Matt Halfpenny found his way onto the sportsdesk at the Worksop Guardian; and Sentence, who cut his teeth on local hospital radio before joining the local radio station Mansfield 103.2, offered another pair of willing and trustworthy hands. It was also a pleasure to give the late Matt Genever the benefit of my experience before he fulfilled a dream of his own by becoming a Stags reporter on Mansfield 103.2. Matt was a devoted fan whose passion for the team was unbridled. I'll never forget the day he turned up for a club press conference with blue and yellow hair, dyed for a charitable cause. Tragically Matt was taken from us in 2008 at the tender age of 30, after losing his battle against a brain tumour.

Another job on my already busy roster was updating Mansfield's Club Call service – a telephone information hub that fans could dial up using one of those 0800 numbers and obtain the latest news at a premium rate. A straightforward task that dovetailed nicely into my other match day commitments, but during one memorable season stopped all press box activity dead in its tracks. Never one to miss a sponsorship opportunity, commercial manager John Slater briefed me with a script promoting a local scaffolding company that I had to read out at the start of each report. Simple enough, I can hear you think, but I ignited a spontaneous round of laughter every time I dialed up to announce: "You're listening to Stags Call, brought to you in association with Tubitt Scaffolding, for the best erection in town …"

Another source of embarrassment was a little technique we referred to as "busking". This happened on the rare occasion that Laila, back in the studio, had been unable to record my off-air description of a goal. This would happen if there was a sudden jam of activity across the grounds, leaving her short of time to spool up the tape machine. Digital recording belonged to the same futuristic era of laptops and wi-fi back then. So imagine my dread when Laila would (only occasionally) break the news across the ISDN line that she had missed the latest goal. That was my cue to re-enact the action as if it was happening live, just so it could be captured on tape for the highlights package later in the show. By the time I began 'busking', the post-goal flurry of activity in the press box had usually subsided, along with the hum of the crowd: just enough for my contrived burst of spontaneous commentary to draw a few sniggers, and one or two raised eyebrows from the press box and the directors' box in front of me.

The press box at Field Mill, situated above the directors' box at the back of the old West Stand, was much more spacious and practical than many I had the misfortune to frequent. But it did have a habit of clouding one's judgement, particularly on a damp or cold evening. You see, the benches were concealed behind large glass panels – without ventilation – which would steam up so badly that it would be impossible to see the action down below. Eventually, the glass was removed – perhaps in a vain attempt to improve the quality of the reporting from within! Another problem occasionally reared its head after night matches when the press box lights – operated from the kitchen below – would be turned off by the last departing member of staff, no doubt blissfully unaware that at least one dedicated press man was still busy phoning over his copy. On more than one occasion I remember fumbling my way down the narrow staircase and banging on the door to be released, with another few paragraphs still to off load and a very real fear that I might be spending the night in solitary confinement.

My last couple of seasons in the job were spent reporting from a temporary press facility in the Bishop Street Stand, directly opposite the main West Stand, whilst the ground was being redeveloped. I was fond of the old Bishop Street Stand, where I had occasionally spectated from over the years just for the sake of a different viewpoint. I was sat on the old wooden benches when full back Barry Foster broke his leg against Portsmouth in the mid-Seventies. The makeshift press box actually offered a good, uninterrupted view without distraction. However, it was far less convenient for obtaining team news and interviews from the newly re-located dressing rooms in the far corner of the Quarry Lane end.

Another regular diary date was Radio Nottingham's Monday night football phone-in, which gave (often disgruntled) fans the chance to air their views. John McGovern would be there to field the Forest calls, and Colin Slater would pick up the points raised about Notts County. It was a popular, enjoyable hour-long programme that not only gave supporters the chance to put their points of view forward but also gave us, the reporters, the opportunity to get our teeth into the issues of the day. It was also useful for keeping in touch with the rest of the sports team, face to face, as much of the time we were in different corners of the country.

Digression: I had been working with Laila for about five years before we finally met face to face. During that time we had worked closely on hundreds of live broadcasts, and had filled in the gaps by chatting merrily about our everyday lives. I felt I knew her pretty well, so it was great to finally put a face to the name at a Radio Nottingham party. It's a little surreal to develop a rapport with a colleague you simply never see, but over the years, I've experienced similar situations with other members of production teams who have been pulling all the necessary strings from central London studios whilst I have been working at the sharp end out in the field.

CHAPTER 17

'GET OFF THE PITCH!'

Nottingham Forest were still among the country's top clubs when they reached the Rumbelows League Cup Final at Wembley in 1992, and I was honoured to be a part of the BBC Radio Nottingham team on duty beneath the Twin Towers. My link with the station had given me the opportunity to co-commentate on several Forest matches, as well as the chance to report on Nottinghamshire County Cricket Club's fortunes from Trent Bridge.

Close to 77,000 fans packed into Wembley on a bright spring afternoon, but none of them had a better vantage point than me. With Martin Fisher presenting our dedicated programme from up in the vast press gallery, and later commentating on the game with Andrew James (nowadays a 'Match of the Day' commentator), I was dispatched to the luscious Wembley turf as pitch side reporter. This offered me a whole new perspective, and what an experience it turned out to be. Before the game, I was happily soaking up the atmosphere and interviewing players from both teams as they strolled out from the tunnel for the customary parading of cup final suits. By chance, a photograph of me interviewing United striker Mark Hughes appeared in a football magazine soon after, but in truth a quite arrogant 'Sparky' was not as obliging as he might have been.

At kick-off, I took my place behind the goal, crouched amid a posse of press photographers, poised to interject the match commentary with regular live viewpoints from pitch level. It was positively electric. The pace of the game and the accuracy and speed of the passing as the glossy white ball zipped about the springy turf was mesmerising. And never had I seen a player move with the ball as sharply as United's livewire Russian winger Andrei Kanchelskis. United, wearing their blue change strip, went on to win the final with a 14th minute strike by Scottish international Brian McClair, and after the game I was perfectly placed to gauge the reaction of the dejected Forest stars.

Among them was striker Teddy Sheringham, who was walking towards me when Martin set up my latest cue. "And now let's go back down to the pitch where Simon has been joined by Teddy Sheringham ..." Stepping onto the hallowed turf with my microphone stuck out in front of me, I began to ask the future England striker the statutory questions. Despite the disappointing result, he began to explain where he felt it had all gone wrong when our live broadcast was interrupted by an abrupt security guard. "Cam' on, awf the pitch," he growled in a Cockney tone, whilst pushing both Teddy and myself across the touchline. Undeterred, I carried on with the interview, describing the actions of the numbskull jobsworth who continued to bark his instructions. The remarkable thing was that as I persisted with my questions, Teddy persisted with his answers – the perfect response to such a rude and ill-timed intervention.

For the record, it was to become Brian Clough's last ever major final as a manager, but merely another step along the path to glory for some of his stars such as Sheringham, Des Walker and Roy Keane. In goal, Andy Marriott added a truly local twist to the final. Andy had grown up in Sutton-in-Ashfield, leaving Arsenal for a dream move to his local club in 1989 for £50,000. However, his time at the City Ground was short-lived and his cup final appearance was one of only 13 for the club before he moved on to a string of others including Wrexham and Barnsley.

Another memorable day with the Radio Nottingham commentary team was Forest's 1991 FA Cup semi-final against West Ham United at Villa Park. It was a momentous occasion amid a rip-roaring atmosphere as Clough's men swept aside the Hammers 4-0 en route to their final defeat by Tottenham. Back then, we had to park up on a side street near the ground and were taken aback when a bunch of scruffy kids promised to look after our radio car in return for a crisp fiver. The protection money was reluctantly handed over before we made our way to the stadium.

Around this time I was fortunate enough to commentate on two Wembley play-off finals for a local company producing commemorative videos for the clubs involved. One of those finals was Notts County's showdown with Brighton and Hove Albion in 1991 for a place in the old First Division. Interviewing the Notts players on the Wembley turf before the game was a great thrill. One of those surreal moments when you take time out to remind yourself where you are and what you are doing: standing in the middle of Wembley Stadium on a beautiful June afternoon, interviewing professional footballers about a high profile game that has attracted around 50,000 excited fans. Later I commentated on the full 90 minutes from a dedicated position high above the halfway line. Notts won 3-1, thanks to a double by that flame haired starlet Tommy Johnson. Dean Yates, later to become Colin Slater's summariser on Radio Nottingham, was also on the team sheet.

The production company called me up for several assignments. The money was poor but unimportant: the experience of working in what was affectively a live television environment at the greatest football stadium in the world, and at other top grounds, was invaluable. However, one such filming session on location didn't exactly go to plan, through no fault of my own. I found myself high up on Primrose Hill in London, about to interview two of Hull City's most celebrated fans for a video about their great goalscoring duo of the Sixties, Ken Wagstaff (the former Stags hero) and Chris Chilton. The film was called 'Waggy And Chillo' and I had already met the legendary duo in another recording session up on Humberside.

Now it was my task to capture the memories of the brilliant actor Sir Tom

Courtenay and illustrious playwrite Alan Plater CBE – both staunch Tigers supporters back in the heady days of Second Division football at Boothferry Park. Alan was famed for works such as 'The Last of the Blonde Bombshells' and 'Oh No, It's Selwyn Froggitt', while Tom had played such masterful roles in films like 'Billy Liar' and 'Dr Zhivago'. Microphone in hand, and standing face to face with Tom, I moistened my mouth and waited for my cue from the cameraman-cum-director. But the cue could not be delivered. Tom gazed at me in anticipation and I gazed at my colleague who was no doubt wishing the ground would swallow him whole. In his haste, a vital cable had been omitted from the kit bag and the interview could not take place. Both stars seemed rather put out by such an untimely error but agreed to reschedule the interview at Alan's flat later in the day. My red-faced colleague drove across London to buy the vital piece of equipment he needed to 'can' the job. It was an embarrassing moment, and somehow took the shine off meeting two television greats. Alan passed away in 2010, but Tom's acting career continues following his knighthood for services to television and theatre in 2001.

It was during these early years with Radio Nottingham that I indulged my love for cricket. On summer Saturdays I would be out and about in the Mansfield area, covering the 'Star Match' for the next edition of the Chad. But it was the BBC who gave me the opportunity to broadcast reports on first class games from one of the greatest venues in world cricket, Trent Bridge. The pinnacle was, beyond question, the day Notts clinched the Refuge Assurance Sunday League title in front of their home crowd on the final day of the 1991 season. I was reporting on the action as it unfolded from a small, white painted wooden press box high up above the pavilion, some years before a new panoramic press centre was built as part of the historic venue's re-development.

For the record, Derbyshire were put in to bat by skipper Tim Robinson and fumbled their way to a modest 176 for nine by the end of their 40 overs – Andy Pick, attached to Clipstone Cricket Club, and the late Mark Saxelby from Newark (who tragically took his own life in 2000) among the wickets. Bruce French contributed with a catch, as did Derek Randall. The great Franklyn Stephenson, an imposing Barbadian, enhanced his popularity by removing the classy Kim Barnett for just six on his way to an economical haul of two for 13 off his maximum eight overs.

It was a target that always looked well within Nottinghamshire's reach and Randall, opening with fellow England international Chris Broad, contributed an entertaining 67. 'Broady' was the real talisman, however, remaining at the crease on 73, with Robinson unbeaten at the other end on 25 as the home side set Trent Bridge alight. This was broadcasting gold dust. Fans swarmed the outfield in front of the pavilion steps to celebrate with their heroes as I described the scenes below. So intense was the chanting and cheering that I simply paused and pointed my lip mic out of the window. For a minute or so the events beneath me told their own story. Notts were Sunday League champions for the first and only time and I was the proud commentator who brought the news to thousands across the airwaves.

By the end of 1992, I had the urge to take my career to a new level and embarked on the freelance career I touched upon earlier. I had been at the Chad for over 10 happy years, and had been sports editor for the past four and a half. But, at 28, it was time to spread my wings if I had any hope of developing my journalistic and broadcasting career. By now I was an experienced football correspondent and had four seasons of live broadcasting on my CV. What I needed was not a complete change, but the flexibility and freedom to develop my media interests. To help pay the bills, I took a part-time role in the Ashfield District Council press office and conveniently swapped sports reporting roles with my opposite number John Lomas.

He was also looking for a new challenge, so slipped seamlessly into the job I had vacated at the Chad. At the same time, John's sports editor Duncan Hamilton happily signed me up as the Nottingham Evening Post's new Stags correspondent. Having taken the sports pages of the Chad as far as I could, I was now getting my teeth into my new role as a sporting news hound on one of the best evening newspapers in Britain at the time. Duncan, who went on to write an award-winning book about his experiences of working with Brian Clough called 'Provided You Don't Kiss Me', headed up a strong team on the city sports desk. Ray Yeomans, Mick Holland and David Stapleton were dyed in the wool journalists, while Eamonn Gavigan's racing page enjoyed a dedicated following. Ian Ladyman, later to become an accomplished football writer for the Daily Mail, was an emerging talent. Other freelance opportunities – some outside the sporting arena – were presenting themselves but I was still very much the voice of the Stags, and had no intention of relinquishing that title for a good few years to come.

In 1992, the sports team at Radio Nottingham had gained well-deserved recognition for its excellent coverage. Sports producer Martin Fisher, Forest reporter Andrew James, the voice of Notts County Colin Slater, Nottingham Rugby Club reporter Neil Highfield and myself travelled by train to the Grosvenor Hotel in London for the Sony Radio Awards. Everyone who was anyone in the world of radio was there and I sat directly behind pint-sized comedian Ronnie Corbett. Imagine our delight, then, when we scooped a bronze award for best radio programme in our category. There was further success for Martin, who received a silver award for best commentator.

But there was more to come. Later that year we secured the silver award at the prestigious New York Festival's Radio Programming and Promotions Awards. The announcement was made at a ceremony at the Sheraton Hotel in the Big Apple, which drew nominations from 1,500 organisations worldwide. As a team, we were rewarded for our excellence in the sports commentary and analysis category. Unfortunately, none of the team was present to receive it. The station's expenses stretched happily to a trip to London, but transatlantic travel was out of the question. Still, these were magnificent, unparalleled achievements for a local radio station and I, for one, was exceptionally proud to have played my part.

CHAPTER 18

IAN GREAVES, MANAGER & MENTOR

Few characters in football could have made a bigger impression on those who worked with them than the late, great Ian Greaves. Myself included. I've already told you what a guiding light he became to me as a young journalist, so when I use the term 'great', I don't use it lightly. Ian was greeted as a saviour when he arrived at Field Mill in 1983, inheriting a club whose very survival in the Football League hung in jeopardy. What he achieved on the field, and the many fine players he achieved it with, has been well documented. What I want to share with you is a personal insight into the man himself.

'Greavesie', quite simply, was an inspiration. A great motivator. A fine man-manager. With him, I was able to develop that all-important working relationship - built on trust - that I alluded to earlier in the book. I helped him write his weekly column in the Chad, and in the match day programme, as well as recording his comments on day-to-day events at Field Mill. He shared with me his frustrations and the names of players he hoped to sign, safe in the knowledge that I would keep his confidence. And, of course, I always did. Stirring it was, too, to re-live his memories of the Munich air crash that claimed the lives of eight of his fellow Busby Babes. It was a quirk of fate that kept him off the squad list, and off that doomed aeroplane on that winter's day in 1958.

As my own career developed alongside his reign at Mansfield, I witnessed first hand some of the highs and lows of his distinguished decades in football. But nothing excited me more than being so close to the action as the great man set about assembling a squad that would not only win him promotion, but would also experience the unlikely taste of Wembley glory. Interest in the club was at an all time low (less than 1,300 watched the Torquay game in December that season) when the silver-haired Greaves replaced former player and one-time local hero Stuart Boam in February 1983. He must have been questioning his judgement when few more than 1,800 beleaguered fans turned up at Field Mill for his first home game in charge, against Chester City.

This footballing architect was faced with a total rebuild, right down to the foundations, and predictably heads rolled before Greaves was able to use his considerable influence to attract quality young players from big clubs. Mark Kearney arrived from Everton and Tony Lowery from West Bromwich Albion – both on free transfers. But youth never prevailed without that vital blend of experience and the addition of former Leicester City and England full-back Steve Whitworth and ex-Newcastle striker Stuart Barrowclough gave the team a more balanced look. But Greaves's best signing, without a doubt, was centre half George Foster on a free transfer from Derby County.

Still, success wasn't immediate and progress was slow, with finishing positions of 19th and 14th in the basement division failing to capture supporters' imagination. Yet despite this, Greaves instilled an inner belief in the Field Mill corridors. A sense that the club was in the hands of a saviour. It was impossible to question his influence or doubt his vision. Goalkeeper Kevin Hitchcock's arrival from Nottingham Forest as the long-term replacement for the retired Rod Arnold, the arrival of winger Kevin Kent from Newport County and the addition of battle-hardened pros Paul Garner, Neil Whatmore, Neville Chamberlain and Keith Cassells, further fortified the squad.

Greaves also identified the need for a new first team coach and the acquisition of future manager Bill Dearden should not be under-estimated. John Jarman was also brought in to develop the youth policy, achieving that remarkable run in the FA Youth Cup. Greaves was well connected and I remember being invited to a coaching session with the goalkeepers by his former Manchester United team mate Harry Gregg. The once great custodian was a survivor of the Munich disaster, when he saved the lives of several stars including Sir Bobby Charlton and Jackie Blanchflower by pulling them free of the burning wreckage. Imagine how uplifting it was for me, never mind the players, to be in the company of such a great man on a low-key afternoon at Field Mill.

By the time the 1985-6 season kicked off, Greaves had fashioned a team he knew he could take into battle with confidence. And what a season it was! The hat-trick former Watford star Cassells fired against Hereford United in that sun soaked August curtain-raiser set the tone, but another four-goal haul against Hartlepool United in the April ensured Mansfield's return to the old Third Division. Cassells scored twice more, but goals from Whatmore and Kent secured the club's third place finish in a final day victory at Halifax. That wouldn't be the only vital goal Kent would claim, of course.

In truth, Greavesie belonged on a bigger stage, so fitting it was that he led his team to Wembley in 1987 for that magnificent penalty shoot-out victory over Bristol City in the Freight Rover Trophy Final. Ian knew better than anyone that Bristol would provide stern opposition, and in centre forward Joe Jordan, had a potential match winner. Jordan, a Scottish international whose toothless persona gave many a defender a scare during his distinguished years with Leeds United and Manchester United, was playing out his career at Ashton Gate but remained his side's biggest threat. Quite simply, he had to be subdued if Greaves and his team were to achieve the unthinkable, and Jordan's might was all but taken care of even before a ball was kicked when the manager summoned his centre-half and captain, Foster, days before the final. He told him bluntly that he was concerned he might struggle to cope with Jordan. The touch paper was lit. Foster predictably rose to the occasion just as Greaves expected, and delivered the type of masterful performance his manager always knew he was capable of.

As many fans are aware, that Wembley triumph was the beginning of the end of Greavesie's reign at Field Mill. Despite the fact that he had declined an offer to manage at a higher level with West Brom, the club didn't invest sufficiently in his achievements and two relegation fights followed. It must have hurt, then, to face a barrage of national media after Mansfield's 6-2 thrashing at the hands of a resurgent Wolverhampton Wanderers at Molineux on 17th December, 1988. Steve Bull's goals were firing the Wolves revival, and their prowess, together with Greavesie's alluring stature, attracted the top football scribes to the game. He had briefly managed Wolves the year before taking the Stags job but had been unable to stave off relegation and was replaced by Graham Hawkins when a new regime took over the cash-strapped club.

An embarrassed, awkward silence, befell the press room when Greavesie - in his trademark long overcoat and drawing on a big cigar - strolled in to face the music. I stood quietly in the background, dictaphone in hand, happy to let the Sunday paper boys fire the opening salvos. I forget who muttered the opening question, which probably went something like: "How do you sum that up, Ian?". But his response was fantastic. "We were f***ing robbed," he quipped with a grin, rolling those deep brown eyes. There was uproar. The tense atmosphere had been pierced by Greavesie's incisive wit, and the national reporters were suddenly more intent on sharing a beer with the defeated manager than barraging him with a list of awkward questions.

As a young reporter, the last thing you need to deal with is the volatility of a moody manager, and I say with all honesty that I never encountered any form of wrath or backlash during Greaves's reign. If he did feel the strain, he kept it well hidden, and on occasions would much prefer to lighten the tone with an impromptu song. You see, in local entertainer Johnnie Singleton, Greaves had a soul mate. A fellow Lancastrian, Singleton helped to run the Mansfield studio for BBC Radio Nottingham as well as having his own pubs and clubs slot on the local station. He would pay frequent visits to the manager's office and it was somewhat amusing to watch them both burst into a rendition of an old crooning classic.

Ian loved his music, particularly the songs of Elton John, and used the Watford chairman's chart hit of the day 'Passengers' to motive his players on the team coach. The boss didn't want any passengers in his team, and would make sure the number was played out loud on the approach to an away ground. "Deny the passenger, who want to get on", sang Elton. "The spirit's free, but you'll always find, passengers stand and wait in line, someone in front and someone else behind, but passengers always wait in line" … The positive reaction it seemed to inspire among his players always made me smile and put a spring in my own step!

By February 1989, Greaves had left the club after winning promotion and leading his team on that amazing journey to the Twin Towers. He never did manage again, but scouted for some of his old friends including Manchester City boss Peter Reid, who had served him as a player at Bolton. Like many who played for him, and worked alongside him, I was saddened by the news of his death early in 2009. At a function soon after to celebrate the anniversary of the club's famous FA Cup win against West Ham United, former Stags Chairman John Almond described Ian to me as quite simply the best manager the club has ever had, together with the mastermind of that great Sixties side, Tommy Eggleston. It was a fitting tribute.

CHAPTER 19

THE GAFFERS

It was February 1989, just before Chad deadline, and once again Stan – now working with me in the sports department on a part-time basis - had helped to line up another back page exclusive. George Foster was about to be named as the replacement for manager Ian Greaves, and we would be breaking the story in true Chad tradition. But Stan wasn't happy. Gathered in club secretary Joe Eaton's office, awaiting George's arrival, chairman John Pratt sought Stan's approval. "What do you think then, Stan," he enquired, perhaps half-anticipating the answer. "It's a retrograde step," barked Stan as a stony silence befell proceedings.

He wasn't impressed. And not because he had anything les than the greatest respect for Foster the player and club captain. Stan had been insistent that Greaves's replacement should be a man of similar experience – the type of appointment he felt was vital to the club's hopes of regaining the momentum so rapidly lost after the Wembley triumph. Stan was concerned that George, as player-manager, would be under far too much pressure to succeed. Would the added responsibility lessen his impact as a lynchpin on the park? And would he have the necessary contacts in the game to bring the right personnel to an ailing squad? Afterall, it wasn't many years ago that Stan had seen another Stags icon, Stuart Boam, crash and burn as a player-manager and here was Foster, about to become the youngest man in the club's long history to hold that position.

In the twilight of an admirable playing career, the red-haired Devonian was hungry for the challenge, and his appointment at least promoted continuity. George had been championed on the terraces from the first time he pulled on the amber jersey, and appeared to possess all the attributes and qualities required to make a successful transition from player to 'gaffer' at some stage. I got on well with him and admired his commitment to the shirt. I hoped he would succeed. However, his relationship with a significant section of the fanbase swung from unbridled love to festering hate over the next four turbulent years. George has the dubious distinction of being the only Stags manager to suffer two relegations, though in between he did lead the club to the Fourth Division Championship in 1992, of course. He was also Manager of the Month in the basement league in the October of his championship season.

To his credit, he guided the club straight back to the newly named League One at the first attempt, but even so, his uneasy relationship with certain factions continued as a sticky March threatened to thwart their promotion charge. By the time The Stags took on Rochdale in a win or bust finale at Field Mill that season, George had already fired a salvo or two back at his tormentors through his columns in the press, pieced together with a hint of diplomacy by yours truly. But after one miserable performance later in his reign, he stood by the mouth of the old West Stand tunnel and gazed coldly into the face of another torrent of abuse. It was an act of self-respect, but such actions only incited his detractors.

So great was his hurt, that when goals by Phil Stant and Ian Stringfellow clinched promotion with that 2-1 win over Rochdale, the spontaneous celebrations that ensued in the West Stand took place largely without him. The players, relieved and euphoric at clinching the third and final promotion spot, climbed the staircase from the dressing rooms to greet what looked like the majority of a 5,600 crowd from the directors' box. But George wasn't among them. Back down in the dressing room, where the chants from above were resonating, the promotion-winning boss remained defiant. "They're calling for you, George," I told him after recording his post-match reaction for BBC Radio Nottingham in a now empty, champagne showered dressing room. But he had no intention of milking the applause. He felt hurt by the way he had been treated and pride was telling him not to join in. I felt for him, but respected his feelings. His was a hollow victory.

With no money to spend to consolidate his achievement in the close-season that followed, the witch-hunt wasn't over. To my mind, the odds were always stacked against him. Another relegation predictably followed and personal morale appeared to be at a submissive low following his apparently reluctant sale of leading scorer Phil Stant (to Cardiff City), whose goalmouth prowess was a prized asset. On 15th July, 1993, the much-maligned Keith Haslam became the club's new owner and George's troubled reign was reaching an inevitable end. New brooms invariably sweep clean, as they say, but it was a surprise when the new chairman wielded his axe just four games into the 1993-94 season, following a 2-0 defeat by Crewe Alexandra. George knew better than anyone that his fate was all but sealed, yet was determined not to willingly turn his back on the challenge. In the end, the financial constraints that led to Greaves's demise ultimately contributed to George's downfall, too.

So why did it all go wrong? It's a fact that he had money to spend initially, before owners Abacus Lighting began to lose the will to continue. And whilst he made mistakes in recruiting new players, don't forget that he also brought in some of the best, including those prolific marksmen Stant and Steve Wilkinson, who certainly justified their respective transfer fees. George was unfairly lambasted by some sections of the crowd for failing to steady a sinking ship and stave off relegation in his first season in charge, even though the end-product was at times woeful. The abuse from some quarters was sickening. The relationship between fans and manager became so strained in that first season that its prospects of reconciliation became untenable.

Looking back, coping with the burden of leading the team as king pin defender and boss in his formative years in the job was a precarious baptism. Player-managers rarely succeed in the long term, and it is hardly surprising when you consider the pressures placed upon them. Back then, George understandably needed the time to concentrate on honing his training ground strategies, as well as developing the necessary man-management skills, watching endless games and cultivating that all-important network of contacts. Despite these challenges, George – a naturally big man - had to work exceptionally hard to maintain a level of fitness that would allow him to live up to the exacting benchmark he had always set himself on the field of play. His decision to bring in his former Derby County boss John Newman as an extra pair of experienced eyes made little impact, so Stan's fears back in 1989 were not completely unfounded. Though I always got on well with George, as a player and a manager, interviewing him after a heavy defeat could be like walking a verbal tightrope and on occasions such reaction was a little hurtful. It wasn't personal, I knew that. A natural-born winner, George wore his bruised heart on an often blood-stained sleeve and the pain of failure was always too much to bear.

Andy King brought an altogether different approach to management when he replaced Foster soon after the arrival of new club owner Haslam in November 1993. King was best known to me for his appearance on the opening titles of 'Match of the Day' every Saturday night, when he was repeatedly bundled off the touchline by a policeman who clearly couldn't differentiate a player from a fan. From the minute I took my front row seat at the press conference to announce his arrival, I warmed to the former Everton midfielder. King was fun-loving and flamboyant: qualities he passed on to his team in their often cavalier style of play. His near three-year term was punctuated with exciting, high scoring games and lively interviews. Perhaps the most off-beat story he created – and one which made the national press – was his apparent signing of former Olympic gold medallist Daley Thompson, who spent a couple of weeks at the club on trial. Already in his late thirties, but still super fit, Thompson seemed genuinely intent on breaking into the team, but in reality King's tongue never came out of his cheek amid speculation that he might make the grade.

'Kingy' and I got on famously. He always had time for me, providing me with newsworthy snippets on a daily basis, as well as sharing a coach seat on those long late night journeys home to pick through his carefully thought out after-match analysis. In return, I championed his cause, along with the fans who were appreciative of his open style when things were going well. There's no doubt in my mind that his crowning moment (forgive the pun) was not achieving a play-off place in the 1994-95 season, but that famous League Cup win against Leeds United at Elland Road early in the same campaign - a game I'll reflect upon in more detail in a later chapter. Andy, like Ian Greaves before him, had spent his career on a bigger stage. He had played at the highest level, and masterminding a 1-0 win against such a big club on their own manor filled him with pride. He positively soaked up the limelight when, with mandatory cigar in hand, he exchanged amusing banter with the national press after the game.

Supported by former Everton coach Colin Harvey, no manager before or since has brought a more attractive, mesmerising brand of football to Field Mill. Between November and January of that season, King's team registered a remarkable string of high scoring victories: 4-3 at Scunthorpe, 4-2 at home to arch rivals Chesterfield, 7-1 at home to Hereford United, 5-2 at Scarborough, 3-0 at home to Barnet, 4-3 at home to Wigan Athletic, and a rousing 3-2 home defeat by Wolves in the third round of the FA Cup.

His judgement was sound when it came to signing promising new talent. Aidy Boothroyd and Ian Baraclough, who both graduated to become talented managers in their own right, were notable additions, along with young guns John Doolan, Simon Ireland and speedball Stewart Hadley. Andy also inspired older players by giving them licence to express themselves. Steve Wilkinson thrived, Iffy Onuora overcame his injury woes to make an explosive contribution, while Steve Parkin grew in stature as team captain. The loan signing of O'Neill Donaldson was also inspired.

Even without Donaldson, whose stay was impactful but short lived, King steered the Stags to the play-offs that season, but the semi-final defeat at Chesterfield (another game I will spotlight) signalled the beginning of the end for him. Haslam's reluctance to invest in better players following the £100,000 sale of Wilkinson to Preston North End and the injuries that curtailed Iffy Onuora's appearances left King short of firepower and his working relationship with Haslam predictably faltered. The fans had directed their frustrations at the chairman so it was somewhat predictable that a lowly finish the following season led to King's sacking early in the 1996-97 campaign.

When Steve Parkin was placed in charge as caretaker in August 1996, he took a step towards becoming the youngest manager in the country when the position was made permanent two months later. Steve always had the credentials to make an excellent coach and manager: he had become an Under 21 international during his time at Stoke City and had been encouraged to work with the youth team during his time as King's club captain. Despite his young age, Steve grasped his opportunity with both hands, quickly gaining the respect of the senior players he had shared a dressing room with on the same level only weeks before. A strong man manager, he was forthright, honest and fair, and quickly combined his motivational skills with a tactical awareness that belied his inexperience. Crucially, he made the wise decision not to play on, but to pour his energies into managing the team. Assisted by the evergreen Tony Ford, his eyes on the field of play, he deserves great credit for getting the club to the fringes of the play-offs in two consecutive seasons.

Conducting interviews on Thursday mornings in readiness for the weekend programme was serious stuff, but every broadcaster falls victim to a fit of giggles at some stage of his career and something Steve said during one recording session set off mine. He, too, saw the humour in what he'd quipped and it must have taken a dozen re-takes before the two of us could compose ourselves long enough to get the job in the can. Sadly, yet somehow predictably, he became disheartened by familiar constraints, and with a transfer embargo imposed on the club, he departed for a new challenge. There is no doubt that Rochdale's gain back then was very much Mansfield's loss.

It is no surprise to see Steve establish himself as a well respected coach, bouncing back from a frustrating spell at a cash-strapped Barnsley to eventually play an influential role as first team coach in Hull City's remarkable rise to the Premier League under Phil Brown a few years ago. Since then Steve, who has produced such exciting top flight players as Grant Holt and Rickie Lambert, has contributed to Bradford City's promotion from League Two – a campaign that took them to Wembley not once, but twice, in the League Cup Final and the play-off final against former Stags team mate Aidy Boothroyd's Northampton Town.

Long-serving coach Bill Dearden deserved his chance to manage a club and returned to replace 'Parky' in 1999. He had been John Rudge's right-hand man at Port Vale since leaving the Stags five years earlier but the opportunity to become the 'gaffer' in his own right was irresistible. Bill's strengths were his wealth of contacts within the game – he was respected as a coach among his peers in all four divisions and beyond - and his ability to nurture young players. He mentored the likes of Liam Lawrence, Lee Williamson and Bobby Hassell, who all went on to play at a higher level. Wayne Corden, a cultured left footed player, and goalscorer Chris Greenacre were others who blossomed in his care.

Bill was in the same mould as Greaves; a no-nonsense Lancastrian who believed in saying it exactly as he saw it. You always knew where you stood with Bill. I understood the difficulties he faced, just as I had understood the constraints imposed on those before him, and the two of us developed a good friendship that had germinated some 15 years earlier when he arrived at Field Mill from Chesterfield and I was finding my feet as a fresh faced trainee reporter. In fact, Bill and his wife Judith were wedding guests when I married my wife Joanne in 1995.

No one could reproach him for accepting the chance to manage neighbours Notts County midway through the 2001-2 season: a better job at a bigger club. He left the team in a strong position and it was coach and former centre half Stuart Watkiss who finished the job by steering the Stags to promotion. Watkiss was a bright young talent in the Parkin mould and instantly knew how to get the best out of senior and junior professionals alike. I admired his openness and supported him in the way I had respected each of his predecessors. We were often ribbed for being lookalikes, so much so that one Saturday the Football Post published mug shots of us both, complete with a witty caption!

It was a red letter day for the former postal worker when he finished the job by clinching promotion with a home win over Carlisle United on the final Saturday of the season. It was a poignant moment for me, too, as it was my last ever match as a Stags correspondent. On reflection it felt almost fraudulent to borrow probably the greatest line in sports commentary to describe the closing scenes, but it appeared on my tongue instinctively and spontaneously. Stags were leading 2-0, and were seconds from promotion when dozens of fans spilled onto the Field Mill turf. "There are people on the pitch. They think it's all over. It is now!" The final whistle had been blown. And it was all over. After re-incarnating Kenneth Wolstenholme's immortal statement and re-living the previous 90 minutes with Watkiss in the temporary Bishop Street press box, it was time to hang up my microphone. Touchingly, Radio Nottingham's sports editor Colin Fray, his assistant Robin Chipperfield and Mr Notts County Colin Slater all paid me an emotional on-air tribute in acknowledgement of 13 years on the airwaves. A new career in television beckoned for me, but for Watkiss troubled waters lay ahead. How could any of us have believed that day that the club would soon begin drifting into catastrophic decline, culminating in relegation from the Football League in 2008. Thankfully that slide towards oblivion has been arrested by the passion and commitment of the team headed by new chairman John Radford, himself a lifelong Stags fan.

On reflection, I genuinely believe that Foster, King, Parkin, Dearden and Watkiss all did as well as could have been expected with such limited resources during a difficult era in the club's history. Like most small clubs, financial constraints have historically stunted Mansfield's progress. There's no doubt in my mind that bolder investment in 1987 might have seen Greaves take the club to a whole new level, just as consolidation might have helped Peter Morris sustain Second Division status under a different regime back in the Seventies.

CHAPTER 20

WATCH OUT, STANTY'S ABOUT

Through two decades of following The Stags I had the privilege of meeting and working with some tremendous footballers and personalities. None, though, entertained me more - on or off the pitch - than popular striker Phil Stant, who became a good friend on arriving at Field Mill from Fulham for £60,000 in February 1991. 'Stanty', affectionately though rather inappropriately nicknamed 'Psycho' by the fans, scored some remarkable goals - 26 of them in the promotion season of 1991-92 - and none more important than the last one against Rochdale that helped clinch that crucial third spot.

Whilst some players became engrossed in those card schools on long away trips, and others read the papers or slept, practical joker Stanty was always on the look-out for mischief. So, as you may imagine, the centre forward was in his absolute element on a never-ending coach trip to Carlisle United in September 1991, when the handle on the toilet door malfunctioned. It didn't take long for Stanty to realise that he could lock its poor, unsuspecting user inside the cubicle with inconspicuous ease.

Predictably, John Lomas became his first victim, and probably spent enough time in there to feel the need to go twice. By now Stanty was cackling with excitement and could barely wait to ensnare another. Now, Carlisle is a good three and a half hours from Mansfield by coach and after consuming a coffee or two en route, I couldn't keep my legs crossed any longer. Reluctantly, but in desperate need of relief, I shuffled forward to hear the click of the door behind me and another round of giggles from the number nine. However, it was coach John Newman who came dangerously close to spending the whole evening locked in the khazi! If it hadn't been for Assistant Manager Bill Dearden returning to the coach for his overcoat on a cool evening, with the team already in the dressing room, poor John - pleading in vain to be set free - would probably have been there all night.

At the height of his career at Field Mill, mobile phones still resembled building bricks and few of us possessed one, as I've already explained. But Stanty knew he could have another laugh at someone's expense when he stuffed his young son Craig's toy mobile into his kit bag. I knew he was up to no good when, after finishing an interview with me in the tunnel area, he flashed me a glimpse of the phone and beckoned me into coach Kevin Randall's office. No sooner had a conversation been struck that the phone began to ring out from inside the bag. "One minute, Kev," muttered Stanty in his engaging Bolton accent. "My agent's on the phone." Reaching into his bag, he pulled out his mobile and began to chat to his mythical agent about some bogus offer from another club. Kevin's expression was unforgettable. I'm still not sure whether he was gobsmacked by the phone, or that fact that Phil had a big-wheeling agent (unusual at that level in those days). Or both!

The tables were turned to some extent when the club's excellent commercial manager John Slater broke the news to Stanty that he had been offered a sponsored car. He was, as footballers say, over the moon, until he discovered that the car in question wasn't the sporty, fuel-thirsty growler that he had probably expected. Believe it or not it was a Skoda, a reliable make but not renowned for being hip and cool. It was great fun attending the photo shoot and even funnier watching him drive it away from the forecourt – for once, without that crafty grin written across his mischievous face.

On the field of play, the former SAS soldier gave his all game in, game out, and the club owed him a huge debt of thanks for the 26 goals that fired them to promotion in 1992. Phil was a natural goalscorer who fed off his own instinct in front of goal. He wasn't blessed with pace, but had a sixth sense when it came to being in the right place at the right time, and it was rare if he didn't finish a goal attempt with pin-point accuracy. He had already earned a reputation for finding the net with some regularity in successful spells with Hereford United and Notts County, so it was no surprise when he became an instant hit at Field Mill. As that promotion campaign reached its climax, none of his goals proved more vital than the hat-trick against Halifax in a 3-2 home win just three games from the end of a nail-biting run-in, or the strike against Rochdale on the final Saturday.

During his time at Field Mill, Phil rarely spoke about his career as a soldier with the 5th Infantry Brigade in the Falklands War, though he occasionally aired the idea of writing an autobiography – an ambition he realised upon hanging up his boots. In the meantime, a frank and revealing interview in the Independent on the 30th anniversary of the conflict in 2012 gave a compelling insight into his mindset as a professional footballer: a side of Phil that I had never delved into nor truly contemplated during his time at Field Mill. Reflecting on the Argentinian attack on two British war ships at Bluff Cove, Phil recalled: "We were the first people there after the strikes. Our NCOs took control of the situation until we got help by the medics, the paras and the marines. When you're seeing people with limbs off and skin melting, people screaming, it's something that you never forget. That's when it wasn't an adventure any more. That was the day I grew up. Nothing was ever the same again but football was always my release and I never stopped appreciating just how lucky I was to be a professional footballer," he said.

"You never forget those times and you are a different person but some guys, unfortunately, when they come back from war don't have that release. I was very lucky that I had football to concentrate on. I went back to the Falklands in 2007 and I didn't realise just how beautiful they were. All that we had seen was a trench, mud, snow and gale-force winds for weeks. It was minus 21 when we were out there – Carlisle on a Tuesday night was never a problem after that." I doubt that John Newman would have agreed from the solitary confinement of that coach loo!

Few players during my time enjoyed such a strong rapport with the fans as Phil. Other prolific goalscorers had graced the Field Mill turf, but without commanding the same level of adoration. Apart from his eye for a goal, he had a warmth and honesty that fans could relate to. Off the pitch, he was on their level and would offer his time to talk freely with them before and after games. He was a joker with a zest for fun, but understood the importance of more serious business when he was required to go back into combat mode.

It could be that no other player has touched the Field Mill faithful like Stant since the great Ken Wagstaff in the Sixties. The burly forward fired 34 goals in 44 appearances in the 1962-63 season and followed up by completing a haul of 29 more in 46 games just weeks before I was born. Ken is to this day a true Mansfield legend, not only because of his goalscoring prowess but because, he, like Stant, was a man of the people.

Ken was the apple of former Stags secretary Joe Eaton's eye. He guided the great player through a mischievous youth and recounted endless stories to me about his protégé over a cup of tea in the Field Mill office over the years. Statistics alone illustrate why he was held in such high regard by everyone involved in the club. The Langwith-born forward was thrust into first team football before his 18th birthday by manager Raich Carter but 93 goals in 181 games tempted Hull City to sign him in 1964 for the princely sum of £40,000. It was money well spent. Ken blasted a further 173 goals in 378 games for the Tigers. He was surely one of the greatest players never to play in the top division, or never to have the honour of representing his country.

Whilst his exploits came before my time, it has been a great privilege to meet him on a number of occasions in recent years, usually on the racecourse. Like me, Ken loves racing, and our paths do cross from time to time at his local track Beverley. The racing world paid him its own tribute in 1968 when a racehorse, 'Waggy', was named after him. I visited his club in Hessle, near Hull, when I interviewed him for the 'Waggy and Chillo' video and soon began to realise that he was worshipped just as much on Humberside as he is in the Mansfield area to this day.

CHAPTER 21

MY 10 MOST AMAZING MATCHES

Over 13 seasons between 1989 and 2002, I covered around 650 Mansfield Town games for BBC Radio Nottingham. During that time, I wrote many more match reports for first the Mansfield Chronicle Advertiser, then the Nottingham Evening Post and it's sister Saturday paper the Football Post. In total, I spent the first 20 years of my journalistic career reporting in some shape or form on the fortunes of the Stags. During that time I witnessed some great games, some very bad ones and lots of indifferent moments in between. Football matches stay in our memories for all sorts of reasons. The experience of watching a game is personal to us all. This compilation of my 10 most amazing matches is not all about the greatest games, the best goals, the biggest occasions. It's about the games that stirred me personally in many different ways.

1. Stags 1 Bristol City 1
(After extra time. Mansfield won 5-4 on penalties)
Freight Rover Trophy Final, Wembley, 24th May 1987

Prior to the inception of the Associate Members' Cup – a knock-out competition for lower league clubs that ran under several different guises – the prospect of seeing The Stags on that hallowed Wembley turf was unthinkable. To be frank, you wouldn't even have dreamed about it. That all too brief flirtation with the old Second Division in the late Seventies was enough to exceed the expectations of most supporters of a club whose history had always been entrenched in the basement divisions. But, in 1987, the unthinkable happened and the Stags were indeed off to Wembley following a near miss two years earlier. The late, great Ian Greaves had built a promotion-winning team to be proud of and a two-leg semi-final victory over Chester City in April had clinched a place in the Freight Rover Trophy Final against Third Division rivals Bristol City. It was, arguably, the biggest thing to happen to the mining town of Mansfield as 25,000 people joined the blue and yellow convoy down the M1 to North London's footballing mecca.

My most notable contribution to the build up to the historic occasion was to pen the front page 'lead' in the Chad just days before the final. Beneath a banner headline of 'Here we go!', I wrote: "Mansfield will become a ghost town on Sunday when more than 20,000 people follow Mansfield Town to Wembley. A convoy of cars and coaches will file down the M1 to cheer on the Stags in their fairytale Freight Rover Trophy final against Third Division rivals Bristol City. On Tuesday ticket sales at Field Mill had already topped the 15,000 mark, with thousands more expected to pay at the Wembley turnstiles ..." I went on to report how the club's coach agents Taggs had already filled 40 buses, bringing in transport from every corner of the county to help meet the demand. Around 1,000 tee-shirts and rosettes had been sold at the club shop prompting proud, long-serving club secretary Joe Eaton to declare: "The telephones have never stopped ringing." No prospect of on-line sales back then!

By now I was an established member of the Chad sports department, writing regular news stories and feature articles on the Stags each week. However, I was only on the subs' bench, so to speak, for this momentous occasion. Tim Morriss, who had succeeded Stan Searl as sports editor, had the honour of writing the match report for the following Wednesday's paper. Stan, helping out on the sports desk on a part-time basis, was still at the helm for BBC Radio Nottingham and was poised to summarise alongside Jeremy Nicholas, who had joined the team to provide live match commentary. On the day, my seat in the press box was reserved to provide some of those all-important incidental story lines. Tim was no stranger to the Wembley press box, having had the great fortune to follow Rainworth Welfare to that famous FA Vase Final in 1982. For all three of us, this was a career pinnacle. Even then, in the fledgling stages of my career, I knew that I was part of something that might never present itself again.

It was awe-inspiring. The march up Wembley Way amid a cacophony of yellow and blue. The biggest ever gathering of Stags fans singing their hearts out in unison beneath those hallowed Twin Towers. And the deafening roar that almost lifted the roof as the distinctive white head of Greaves emerged from the tunnel to our left, his chest swollen with pride as he led his gladiators onto that famous old turf. How smart he looked in his blue blazer and yellow button hole. Stan's voice faltered at the sight as a tear welled in his eye. The lump in my throat was difficult to swallow, but my emotions weren't on public display. Reaching Wembley was heady stuff, but had any of us dared to think that the Stags might just lift the trophy? Bristol City represented formidable opposition. Any team that reaches a cup final does so on merit, but this team was robust and experienced, and had won this competition 12 months earlier. What's more, they were no doubt riled by that 2-0 League defeat at Field Mill about six weeks earlier.

When Kevin Kent swept Mansfield into a 57th minute lead the belief on the terraces that glory could indeed be theirs began to grow. The Stags were on top, City were ruffled, and it could have been 2-0 when young substitute Ian Stringfellow headed against the crossbar soon after. Everyone in yellow and blue hoped, quietly, that it wouldn't be a costly near miss. Foster continued to beat former Scottish international Jordan to just about every aerial battle while Kevin Hitchcock in the Mansfield goal pulled off an amazing save to deny David Moyes (a future top manager and Sir Alex Ferguson's successor at Manchester United, of course).

The Stags repelled City's retaliation for 87 minutes before one half of Wembley's

58,586 crowd was stunned to silence. Hitchcock was finally beaten but little did we know that he would shortly be exacting his own revenge in a nail-biting penalty shoot-out. Extra time couldn't produce a winner and it seemed so unjust when Stags striker Keith Cassells – a hero all afternoon – missed his spot kick to leave City just one penalty away from retaining the trophy. Thankfully, Hitchcock denied Gordon Owen with his legs before Kent stepped forward to make it 4-4 as the tie moved into a nail-biting sudden death. Remarkably Hitchcock thwarted City again. The tension was unbearable – I can feel my stomach churning all over again as I re-live it now – as defender Tony Kenworthy placed the ball on the spot. Standing between 'TK' and immortality was his former Sheffield United team mate Keith Waugh, but the wily number six sent the goalkeeper the wrong way. It was over! The Stags were Wembley heroes.

2. Leeds United 0 Stags 1
League Cup Second Round, First Leg, 21st September 1994

Under manager Andy King, Mansfield had honed a flamboyant, open style of play that was exciting to watch and yielded a plentiful supply of goals. Victory over Rochdale in the two-legged first round netted them a plum draw against top flight giants Leeds United – a tie that held special significance for me as a boyhood Leeds fanatic. The prospect of broadcasting from Elland Road filled me with excitement, but it was the eventual outcome that really had my heart racing.

Unsurprisingly, Radio Nottingham decided to give the tie top billing. It would be a full commentary game, with injured Stags striker Iffy Onuora agreeing to sit in as my expert analyst on the night. As usual, I travelled to the tie on the team coach and shared the tension during the pre-match get-together. The affable striker was a natural in front of a microphone, and was always good value for an interview, or a few lively quotes for the newspaper. So, when The Stags were drawn to face Leeds he was the perfect choice to sit alongside me as match summariser. Together, we kicked and headed every ball as Simon Ireland clinched a famous 1-0 victory. Iffy's analysis was incisive, his tension infectious. It was the most exciting game I ever had the pleasure to commentate on, thanks in no small part to my special guest.

The majesty of this great stadium had intimidated many a player over the years, and although Leeds weren't exactly emulating those glory days of the Seventies, they were still a big club with a big reputation and massive expectation. Lowly Mansfield were an obstacle they expected to overcome with the minimum of fuss: a comfortable home win and a professional lock-out at Field Mill two weeks later the game plan. On the contrary, the Stags held Leeds to a goalless stalement in the return leg to progress to round three and a rather anti-climactic 2-0 defeat to Millwall. A lovely footnote to this story arose the day after the Leeds victory when I visited a friend's house and walked past a car that was being polished with its radio on full blast. In its cassette deck was a recording of my commentary the night before. I smiled wryly as I walked past.

3. Middlesbrough 4 Stags 4
League Cup First Round Second Leg, 3rd September 1985

I've already explained the significance of this game to my blossoming career, but it still warrants its place in my top 10 for its sheer entertainment value and its status as a giant killing performance. The cutting from the Chad that week was glued firmly into my scrap book and tells the story perfectly. I wrote: "Mansfield Town's mission at Ayresome Park on Tuesday night was to blot out a frantic Middlesbrough attack and preserve their two-goal first-leg advantage. But instead they found themselves playing the starring role in a nail-biting display of blistering cup-tie action …" Not bad eh? The boy had potential.

In fact, the Stags fired three goals in the space of just four minutes to, as I put it, "claw themselves back from the brink of a first-half disaster." Boro' made their intentions clear with a four-pronged attack that needed only 20 minutes to wipe out Mansfield's first leg advantage. Gary Pollard headed past his own goalkeeper Hitchcock before David Currie elegantly slotted away the second. But half-way through the first half the unthinkable happened. The Stags went goal crazy, as first Mark Kearney converted Neil Whatmore's flick from a Tony Lowery cross. Then right-back Mike Graham made a rare venture over the half-way line to equalise following a clinical one-two with Cassells.

Classy striker Cassells sprung an unconvincing off-side trap to set up Mansfield's third goal of the game, tucked away by Neville Chamberlain from a tight angle, and it was 3-2 on the night, and 5-2 on aggregate. Boro' weren't finished, however, and Gary Rowell netted twice to pull it back to 5-4 overall and set up a tense finale. Despite the pressure of the home side's "galloping legions", the Stags refused to sit behind a defensive barricade and could have extended their lead. Whatmore, Cassells and Mick Vinter all squandered chances with only the 'keeper to beat, but it was Vinter who netted in the dying seconds to level the tie at 4-4 and confirm a second round money spinner against Chelsea thanks to a 6-4 aggregate advantage. For the record, Mansfield held the Blues to a 2-2 draw at Field Mill before going down to a respectable 2-0 defeat at Stamford Bridge – a game I didn't attend.

4. Stags 7 Scunthorpe United 0
Division Four, 21st April 1975

Manager Dave Smith deserved great credit for transforming his team's fortunes so quickly. He had been in the hot seat little more than a year when the Stags confirmed themselves Fourth Division champions with an exhibition performance against poor Scunthorpe United. It was the club's first championship in their 44 years as a Football League club, and what a way to celebrate! Watching from my regular spot just to the right of the tunnel on the lower West Stand terrace, I witnessed the most one-sided match I have ever seen in over 40 years as a football fan.

By half time, the Stags were 2-0 to the good thanks to goals by Ray Clarke and Gordon Hodgson in an overwhelming seven-minute spell. Yet despite the dominance, none of us in the ground could have predicted the avalanche that was to follow. It took Terry Eccles only four minutes to score the third after the break, but 24 minutes passed before the Iron finally buckled – in spectacular fashion! John Lathan crashed in the fourth, with a little help from Eccles, before Clarke got the party started with just 13 minutes of normal time remaining. Lathan got his second soon after, then Kevin Bird completed the demolition in the 86th minute to secure a title that was richly deserved. Looking back, it's worth noting that the Stags occupied top spot from the second week in September, apart from a brief spell when FA Cup commitments saw them fall behind with their fixtures.

There was a slightly sad footnote to the celebrations that evening, however, for on the losing side was former Stags hero Dudley Roberts, who was playing out his career at The Old Showground. I couldn't help but spare a thought for the former Stags cup hero who must have been counting down the minutes. Like many Stags fans, I've since ribbed Dudley about that unfortunate homecoming. He remembered it only too well, but shrugged it off in the best possible manner - with a philosophical grin.

5. Stags 2 Rochdale 1
Division Four, 2nd May 1992

By the time Rochdale arrived at Field Mill for the final game of the season, stuttering Mansfield's hopes of promotion depended on victory and three crucial points. Phil Stant's hat-trick in an edgy 3-2 win over Halfiax Town had been followed by a stalemate at Maidstone United, leaving their fate in the lap of the gods. Victory meant the Stags could rob neighbours Rotherham United of second spot if they slipped up at home to Chesterfield, while Blackpool knew that a win at Lincoln City would see them promoted at the expense of Mansfield if results went their way.

Close to 6,000 chewed finger nails in unison as Rochdale held George Foster's side 0-0 at the interval. The news from Sincil Bank was encouraging, though, as Matt Carmichael had fired The Imps into an early lead. Early into the second half, the prospect of an instant return to the Third Division improved significantly when Ian Stringfellow broke the deadlock. Then, with only 17 minutes of normal time remaining, I exploded into commentary as Stant gave the Stags a two-goal cushion.

Over at Millmoor, Rotherham were battling out a 1-1 draw with Chesterfield after taking a first half lead – a result that was about to clinch them second spot over the Stags by virtue of goal difference. But the tension was cranked up a few more notches when Rochdale pulled a goal back in the closing minutes. At Sincil Bank, Lincoln were still suppressing Blackpool, and courtesy of a few thousand transistor radios, prompted the biggest roar of the afternoon when Carmichael tucked away a late penalty to finally condemn the Seasiders to the play-offs. The drama made great live radio and for that reason it rates right up there with the Leeds tie as a favourite commentary game.

6. Stags 5 Birmingham City 2
Division Three, 3rd April 1990

The headline in the Chad said it all. "SUPER STEVE – Five-goal Wilkinson gives Brum the blues." Only the great Ken Wagstaff had scored more goals for the club than Steve Wilkinson by the time he took his tally to 91 in the 1994-95 season, but this five-star performance in his first season against promotion-chasing City was a career highlight. In typical modesty, Wilkinson played down his haul, claiming in an interview with me that he had played much better in previous starts as a "team man". This was just what the Stags needed to ease their relegation woes, however. 'Wilko' banged home his hat-trick in the space of just 40 minutes, needing only three of those to get off the mark as he swept a right-foot lob over Martin Thomas from 25 yards.

Trevor Christie set up his 12th minute second from close range, before David Hodges helped him force an error out of defender Vince Overson for goal number three. Wilkinson had the City defence in knots at this stage, and when Overson and Trevor Matthewson both attempted to clear the same ball, the predator pounced for his fourth of the night and his 15th of the season with only 42 minutes on the clock. Wilkinson, who would eventually overtake Stags legends Ted Harston and Roy Chapman in the scoring table, had to wait until eight minutes from the end to net his fifth. This time Steve Charles delivered an incisive pass into the striker's path that was dispatched low and hard inside the diving Thomas's right-hand post. At £80,000, he became Mansfield's most expensive signing when George Foster plucked him from Leicester City in October 1989 but it was money well spent. He went on to join Preston North End for a bargain £100,000 in 1995.

7. Stags 1 Wigan Athletic 1
(Wigan won 3-1 on penalties)
Freight Rover Trophy Northern Area Final, 20th May 1985

Though this game ended in agonising defeat, it makes it into my top 10 for the sheer drama and rip-roaring excitement it conjured on an emotion-charged night. Two years before the Stags finally achieved their Wembley dream, the club found itself just 90 minutes away from an historic appearance at the world's most famous stadium. Wigan were the underdogs in this one-off tie, and kick-off had to be delayed by about 15 minutes to allow a crowd of over 9,000 to pack into the stands.

This was a classic cup tie, full of tension, anticipation, ecstasy – and ultimately agony. It was the proverbial rollercoaster, with The Latics taking an early lead when Tony Kelly's harmless shot was deflected into his own net by Stags skipper Foster. But, with only 40 seconds of normal time remaining, Foster redeemed his misfortune with a true blockbuster. Whatmore wriggled past two defenders before picking out Foster with an incisive pass from out wide. Then, without hesitation, Foster powered an unstoppable 25-yard piledriver past the hapless Roy Tunks in the Wigan goal.

So, the tie moved into a nervous penalty shoot-out, but the Stags blew it as Tunks saved their first three penalties by Steve Whitworth, Vinter and then Whatmore. At the other end, Hitchcock did pull off one save, but it was all in vain as Wigan clinched their Wembley place. Little did we know that two years later, the memories of this tortuous defeat would be erased in the most spectacular of circumstances.

8. Stockport County 6 Stags 3
League Cup First Round Second Leg, 26th August 1997

Another defeat, but this Coca Cola Cup tie stands out in my memory as a remarkable game of football. Not only was it a nine-goal feast, but as I wrote in my match report in the next day's Evening Post, "this rip-roaring tie had more twists and turns than a Hitchcock thriller." The Stags had a second round place in the palm of their hands, having won the first leg 4-2 at Field Mill courtesy of a hat-trick from the enigmatic Iyseden Christie. Stockport boss Gary Megson suggested in his programme notes that the previous year's semi-finalists had a mountain to climb, and those comments looked even more valid when Christie fired his team into a 14th minute lead. It was 5-2 on aggregate.

Cup football has always had a habit of conjuring the unexpected, and Stockport hadn't once troubled goalkeeper Ian Bowling when Scott Jones was harshly penalised for bringing down Brett Angell inside the box in the 28th minute. County tucked away the spot kick and Mansfield's advantage was pegged back to two. Then, on the stroke of half-time, Angell powered a header past Bowling to make it 2-1 to the home side on the night, and 5-4 to the Stags across the two legs.

All of us in the Stags camp were only too aware that a 3-1 scoreline in favour of the home side would be enough to see them through on the away goals rule, and they were very much in the ascendancy in pursuit of that killer goal by the interval. Predictably, then, it was advantage Stockport when defender Mike Flynn headed home in the 67th minute. But before the travelling fans had had chance to bury their contorted faces in their amber scarves, the Stags were back in front.

Scouser John Doolan curled home a superb 25 yarder within a minute of County's crucial breakthrough and suddenly it was 3-2 to Stockport on the night but 6-5 to the Stags on aggregate. It was time to get the calculators out as further goals were inevitable. Both sides slugged away like two old heavyweight prize fighters but it was County who drew blood next. This time Alun Armstrong evened things up at 6-6 in the 71st minute. It was 4-2 on the night to Megson's marauders. Mansfield were on the ropes, but this side had a certain spirit and the ability to conjure a goal from out of the blue. Few, however, would have nominated veteran assistant manager Tony Ford as the man to make the next critical breakthrough.

With just seven minutes of normal time left, 'Fordy' stroked an inch-perfect shot into the bottom corner. Just in case you're struggling to keep up, let's take another look at the scores on the doors. It's now 4-3 to Stockport on the night, and 7-6 to the Stags overall.

Surely Mansfield were through. All they had to do was hold their nerve for a few precious minutes. I began preparing my back page introduction for the next day's paper. 'Ford is Stags cup hero' may well have been the headline. But then Bowling failed to deal with a desperate cross and substitute Andy Mutch brought his team level. It was 5-3, and extra time was beckoning, but how would our nerves hold out? The tension in the press box and on the terraces was probably more intense than the pressure on the pitch.

The referee cranked up the atmosphere to boiling point when he added on a few minutes of stoppage time, and Stags defender Scott Eustace almost swung the tie back in Mansfield's favour when he had a header cleared off the line. Unbearable! Then, deep into stoppage time Stockport dealt the Stags the cruelest of all blows. Substitute Kevin Cooper became the unlikely hero when he shot past Bowling to make it 6-3 and 8-7 on aggregate. I had just experienced the most pulsating, nerve-jangling cup tie I had seen since that Middlesbrough game over a decade earlier – and the outcome was crushing, though unforgettable. The Stags had put seven goals past a First Division outfit in two legs but would still not progress.

9. Stags 6 Lincoln City 2
Division Three, 11th March 1995

There was something about Iffy Onuora that was simply irresistible. Intelligent and entertaining off the field, fast and captivating on it, the lively striker was as injury prone as he was brilliant during his checkered two-year career at Field Mill. Born in Scotland to Nigerian parents, I'd first seen Iffy steaming through the Stags defence in a Huddersfield Town shirt a few seasons before Andy King signed him in the close-season of 1994.

It was during one of those spells on the sidelines that he sat beside me during that famous cup win at Elland Road. He had broken a toe in a pre-season friendly at Worksop Town and had been sidelined for six months, but his long-awaited full debut in an amber shirt could not have been scripted more imaginitively. With the Stags in the thick of the promotion race, Onuora was as good as a key new signing to King when he was called up to face local rivals Lincoln City at Field Mill on the crucial run-in - and smashed a quickfire hat-trick!

It was a low key debut for much of the game, so much so that a jaded Iffy later revealed he was preparing to be substituted midway through the second half. Surprised he was, then, when King beckoned Ireland to the bench instead with 67 minutes on the clock. Stags were struggling to prise open a 1-1 stalemate when King played his trump card. Within eight minutes of entering the fray, substitute Stewart Hadley blasted the home side back in front. But what happened next was incredible. Hadley proved the perfect foil for Onuora, who had fresh life pumped into his tiring limbs when the striker teed him up for his first Stags goal in the 78th minute. It was 3-1. Then, in the 83rd minute, Onuora struck again, this time after latching onto a Kevin Lampkin throughball. 4-1. But two minutes later his dream hat-trick was complete when he beat goalkeeper Andy Leaning from the edge of the box. There was more to come from rampant Mansfield. Kevin Noteman made it 6-1 from the penalty spot in the 89th minute before The Imps netted a consolation. On the final whistle, Onuora grabbed the matchball off the referee and later got it signed by his admiring team mates. It was his first ever League hat-trick, and all in the space of seven minutes.

10. Stags 1 Southampton 3
League Cup Second Round, Second Leg, 26th September 2000

Les Robinson, brought to the club as a raw boned youth by Bill Dearden in the Greaves era, was in his second spell with the Stags and in the twilight of his career when he found himself pitched into a hilarious head to head with the great Southampton and England striker Matt Le Tissier in an unforgettable League Cup tie at Field Mill. The Saints had won the first leg 2-0 at The Dell just six days earlier and were on their way to a 3-1 follow-up when play was rudely (yes, rudely!) interrupted by a streaker, who skipped into the centre circle in all his glory, much to the amusement of the crowd. The police were quick to apprehend the frolicking fan, who was promptly escorted back to the touchline so that play could resume.

Robinson was closest to the incident and after the game revealed to me a twist to the tale (forgive the pun!) that must go down in history as a football first. Believe it or not, our streaker had dropped his mobile phone on the field of play and the quick thinking Stags skipper picked it up and tucked it into his shorts, intending to give it back to its owner once the final whistle had blown. A kind gesture, no doubt. But what happened next could not have been scripted. Within minutes of the re-start, Robinson found himself charging towards the Quarry Lane goal in pursuit of a throughball, with the menacing Le Tissier breathing down his neck. The two players were almost shoulder to shoulder when the phone starting to ring – from inside Robinson's shorts! It was our streaker's mate, checking up on his whereabouts after seeing him depart the ground arm in arm with the local constabulary.

Le Tissier, sensing that Robinson was struggling to deny him a goalscoring opportunity, must have been momentarily distracted but, quick as a flash, quipped something like: "I didn't think you'd need to phone a friend, Les," making reference to the lifeline offered to contestants on the TV quiz show 'Who Wants to be a Millionaire?' Fortunately, Robinson did get to the ball first, without any form of assistance, though Southampton won 3-1 on the night. Needless to say, the big-hearted Robinson re-united the grateful streaker with his phone – and his embarrassed mate – after the game.

Le Tissier's god-like status on the Southampton terraces has been well documented, but before kick off in that first leg tie at The Dell, I saw for myself the reaction the great man inspired even before a ball was kicked in anger. It was during the pre-match warm-up that en masse, the Saints fans behind the goal to my left bowed in unison with arms aloft as Le Tissier jogged towards the goalmouth. Another legend in the true sense of the word.

CHAPTER 22

10 MORE GAMES TO FORGET

1. Wrexham 1 Stags 0
Autoglass Trophy Preliminary Round, 15th October 1991

Picture the scene. The Stags are away to Wrexham in the preliminary round of the Autoglass Trophy. It's a cold autumn evening at the vast yet decaying international stadium the Racecourse Ground, and little more than 600 fans have bothered to turn out for such an unispiring clash. The newspaper reporters, among them the Post's John Lomas, huddled behind press benches in the lower half of the main stand, many rows beneath the designated point for the BBC. Having departed the team coach, and acquired my pass, I clambered up the empty steppings to take my place at the radio position for the game.

To my left was the only other incumbent of the BBC Wales facility, a quiet chap who was covering the game for a Welsh speaking audience. With no fans anywhere near us, the occasion lacked atmosphere. Any sense of being at a live cup tie was stilted, to say the least. As well as broadcasting regular reports for Radio Nottingham, I was also phoning copy back to the office for the following morning's edition of the Chad. The game began quietly, and Mansfield were holding their own until Wrexham forged ahead in the first half.

Then, after the break, the Welshmen celebrated again when the ball was lashed into the roof of the net from all of 30 yards by midfielder Andy Preece. Goal! It was a cracker, and determined to commit my description of it to the airwaves, I scribbled down the goal time on my notepad and, head down, began to rant into my handset. It was 2-0 to Wrexham, I informed my listeners, before dialing up my assistant Gordon Foster back in Mansfield to dictate the details in a few more concise paragraphs.

The game was soon over and my reports for radio and print were concluded. The Stags had lost 2-0 I concluded, and were out of the cup. The dream of a return to Wembley was over for another year. But little did I realise that I had made a glaring mistake. The most calamitous mistake any football reporter could ever have the misfortune to make. I'd got the score wrong! Mansfield were definitely not going to Wembley, but they had been beaten by only the solitary goal, not two.

In my haste to report the goal that wasn't, I had taken my eye off the game for a fleeting moment as the referee had ruled out the goal for an infringement. By the time I had lifted my head and re-focused on the action, the Stags had taken the free kick and play had re-started. It was still 1-0. My Welsh speaking colleague surely could have politely corrected me, but didn't, and I certainly wouldn't have picked up on my blunder from his native narratives.

All the way back from Wrexham on the team coach – the best part of a three-hour journey – I was quietly convinced the Stags had been beaten by two goals. Not once did it crop up in conversation, as banter and idle chatter centred around other more interesting topics. So, I drove home from Field Mill, and climbed into my warm bed, blissfully unaware of the calamity that would ensue the following morning.

First to break the news was my great friend John Slater, the club's commercial manager, who could barely inform me of my blunder for laughter. He had turned to the back page of the Chad over breakfast and almost choked on his cornflakes as he glanced down at the match report. The sports desk at Radio Nottingham was next to revel in my embarrassment. I must have been the only reporter ever to attend a football match and get the result wrong – in print and on air. Some double! What's more, I must have been the perpetrator of a thousand office arguments that morning. Thank goodness that my blunder didn't wrongly reflect the actual outcome. Imagine, for example, if the Stags had scored twice, and I'd reported the scores at 2-2 approaching full time ...

In mitigation, I'm hoping you agree that it was wholly forgivable. There I was, isolated from the main body of the media with only an unsociable Welsh speaking radio reporter for company. No fans anywhere near me to alert me with a moan, groan or objection. And the unavoidable need to occasionally take my eye off the game to phone over my simultaneous reports. Forgiven, of course, but a gaff I still get reminded about on occasions. For that reason, the Wrexham tie is most definitely my most forgettable game.

2. Chesterfield 5 Stags 2
Division Three Play-off Semi-Final Second Leg, 17th May 1995

Andy King's idea of relaxing his players ahead of this do or die tie was to take them to a health spa for the day. The semi-final was perched on a knife edge following a 1-1 draw at Field Mill and the boss was intent on easing the tension in the camp. Saltergate was packed to the rafters. Even the cramped wooden benches of the old press box were all accounted for. The road outside the main stand was a sea of blue and amber as both sets of supporters descended on the stadium for the sell-out derby – the prize a Wembley appearance against Preston's victors Bury.

My evening didn't get off to the best of starts when I discovered I had only been allocated one seat in the press box, despite requesting a second for a colleague. Making a case for his admission was daunting, to say the least, as Chesterfield's chairman Norton Lea had assumed control of the chaotic office and was snapping his various disapprovals at anyone within ear-shot. Thankfully, I managed to get the two passes I required and established contact with Nottingham well before kick-off, setting the scene and colouring in the atmosphere for those listening at home. Something told me this was going to be another one of those rollercoaster nights, and my intuition certainly didn't let me down.

When the tie went into extra time at 2-2, the Stags were officially just 30 minutes from Wembley, as the away goals rule gave them the advantage. They had twice taken the lead, through Paul Holland and then Steve Wilkinson, only to allow future Stags striker Tony Lormor and Jonathan Howard to equalise. But even before extra time began, Mansfield's prospects had taken a serious blow with the sending off of steely midfielder Kevin Lampkin. He had been booked on the stroke of half-time but looked harshly treated when Gloucester referee Clive Wilkes pulled the red card from out of his pocket 11 minutes from the end of normal time. His challenge on Nicky Law was wholesome but no worse than several that had gone unpunished before it. Nevertheless, the decision was to change the game – in Chesterfield's favour.

They had their setbacks too, though. Former Stags goalkeeper Andy Beasley was stretchered off with a fractured cheekbone after colliding with Law and Stags striker Stewart Hadley in the 75th minute. I was concerned for Andy, who had been a good pal during his Mansfield days, sharing my passion for a day's racing. His replacement, the former Burnley stopper Billy Stewart, looked nervy and almost gifted Steve Wilkinson a last-gasp winner before the game went into extra time. With a man down, and leaden limbs beginning to falter, the Stags' resistance was breached just five minutes in when Law swept a penalty past Darren Ward. It was 3-2. But the tie really began to spiral out of their grip when Mark Peters followed Lampkin down the tunnel. Law's second goal followed quickly and Howard headed a fifth just five minutes before the end.

In truth, it was rough justice on the Stags and their manager King, having matched The Spireites in every department across the two legs. The headline on the back page of the Evening Post summed it up: "HEARTBREAK – Stags brave bid for Wembley ends in tears." In a post-match interview, King described the pain perfectly. "When the hurting stops, the hard work begins," he told me. Little did he know that he wouldn't get a second bite at that cherry …

3. Wolves 6 Stags 2
Division Two, 17th December 1988

There was a strong moral to this story: If you're struggling, don't plan your club's Christmas party on the day you're playing away to the best team in the division. The official Mansfield Town festive bash was scheduled to take place at Mansfield Brewery as soon as the players returned from Molineux, and I was invited. It was a nice venue at the former Littleworth site, with a tempting buffet supper and a disco laid on. But no one was in the mood for a knees up after a humiliating 6-2 defeat.

The party was more like a wake. So much so, it would have been rude to crack a smile. The raging Steve Bull, aided and abetted by his strike partner Andy Mutch, ran riot for Graham Turner's side, who were emerging from one of their familiar declines with renewed hope and vigour. Stags snatched two consolation goals, courtesy of Simon Coleman and Graham Leishman, on a dark afternoon in the heart of the Black Country. Looking back, it was a death knell for proud boss Ian Greaves, who handled the situation with humour and dignity, as described in an earlier chapter. He would no longer be at the helm when the Stags somehow exacted revenge with a 3-1 win at Field Mill in the return fixture the following April.

4. Luton Town 7 Mansfield Town 2
League Cup Second Round, Second Leg, 3rd October 1989

Stags faced a formidable task against then First Division Luton Town over two legs, so it was imperative to take a good result to the plastic pitch at Kenilworth Road for the return. They twice surrendered the lead at Field Mill and then succumbed to a late goal, but were still in the tie at 3-4. However, injuries threatened to compromise their prospects even before a ball was kicked in the second leg. Manager George Foster had to completely re-shape his back four, which included 17-year-old trainee Kevin Gray. By contrast, The Hatters boasted such talent as Danish international Lars Elstrup and South African striker Roy Wegerle, who took the beleaguered Stags apart with a clinical arrogance.

Elstrup, who had scored twice in the opening leg, fired a hat-trick, and Wegerle added two to his brace at Field Mill. In truth, Luton should have reached double figures – it was that one-sided. Both strikers missed sitters while David Preece and Tim Breacker should have hit the net. And when the home side did find the target, Stags 'keeper Andy Beasley rose to the occasion to avert further disaster.

"STAGS SWAMPED" was my headline in the next morning's Chad, above a scathing paragraph of quotes from red faced boss George Foster. "We came to Luton thinking we could stroll around and get the result we needed without working for it," he told me. "They've scored 11 goals in this tie, but nine of them must have been gifted to them by sloppy defending and bad back passing." George, who probably said something similarly damning in a brief interview with me on Radio Nottingham, was in no mood to spend a minute longer than he needed to at Kenilworth Road and had my colleague John Lomas and I fumbling to finish our reports in fear of being left behind by the team coach.

5. Stags 0 Carlisle United 1
FA Cup Round Five, 15th February 1975

Goals by Ray Clarke and Jimmy McCaffrey at Bury clinched the Stags a place in the fifth round for only the fourth time in their history, and although it wasn't a glamorous tie, their home game against First Division Carlisle United had a winnable look. Sadly, the Stags, still remembered for their FA Cup exploits inside the previous decade, just couldn't capitalise.

Field Mill was packed tight with 18,293 fans – 5,000 of them from Cumbria. It was the biggest attendance since the famous Leicester City quarter-final tie six years earlier. Unfortunately, I wasn't among the crowd so had to agonise over the televised highlights on 'Match of the Day'. By chance, the game the BBC intended to feature – Derby County versus Leeds United – had been postponed so the cameras were re-routed to North Nottinghamshire to offer those of us who didn't have a ticket the chance to savour the action, albeit some hours after the event.

The game itself was no classic. The Stags had their chances, but let themselves down with some questionable finishing. In the end a first half goal was enough to send United through. History books tell me it was striker Bobby Owen who scored the decisive goal, but the one Carlisle player I associate with that tie is journeyman midfielder Ray Train, with his distinctive, tight curly locks. Train went on to play for Sunderland, Bolton Wanderers and Watford, and interestingly scored on his debut at Vicarage Road in a 1-1 draw in December 1978 – against the Stags!

6. Stags 3 Sheffield United 4
Division Three, 22nd September 1979

If Harry Haslam, father of future Stags chairman Keith Haslam, had had his way, the great Diego Maradona would have been entertaining the Field Mill faithful on a warm September afternoon in 1979. Haslam had tabled a £400,000 bid for the young striker from Argentinos Juniors, but when that was rejected the Sheffield United boss turned to a young man by the name of Alex Sabella. The River Plate star arrived at Bramall Lane in the summer of 1978 to add flair to United's promotion push and was proving quite a crowd puller in the Second Division when the Blades descended upon Mansfield.

The game was a cracker. A seven-goal thriller. Sabella, resplendent in his red and white stripes, danced all over the Stags defence but my enjoyment was ruined by an eruption of hooliganism early in the game. Having caught the bus to town with a group of mates to watch the game, I had been enjoying the action along with the majority of an 11,000 crowd when fighting broke out all around us. A group of United fans had infiltrated the North Stand. Punches were flailing and the police and stewards were overwhelmed. The only safe place to be was on the pitch. Frightened and in panic, I leapt over the boundary wall to escape the violence, along with other youngsters who were equally concerned for their safety. Calm was soon restored but the tense atmosphere made it difficult to concentrate on enjoying the game. Watching my back became more of a priority than watching the action on the pitch. It was the closest this 15-year-old had ever come to being directly affected by the hooligan culture that blighted the game in the Seventies.

There had been other moments. I recall being trapped under a shower of rocks that Reading fans were pelting down on the home crowd in the corner of the West Stand, adjacent to the old Quarry Lane terracing, in the mid-Seventies. And sprinting down a busy Lincoln street to avoid a stampede of blood thirsty Imps fans after a typically tense derby at Sincil Bank in the same troubled decade.

7. Stags 2 Matlock Town 5
FA Cup Round Two, 15th December 1976

Mansfield were already rampaging to the Fourth Division championship when local non-leaguers Matlock Town arrived at Field Mill for a second round FA Cup tie. Dave Smith's boys had disposed of Huddersfield after a first round replay and were now surely one simple step away from the chance of securing a lucrative third round tie against a big club. Matlock, though, had other ideas. The neighbouring Northern Premier League club might have considered the wintry weather to be in their favour, as the tie had twice been postponed that week due to frost. Poor conditions, as they say in football, can be a leveller, and what ensued was nothing short of unbelievable.

Matlock, known affectionately as the Gladiators in deepest Derbyshire, took a shock lead when one of three brothers in the side, Nick Fenoughty, chested down a throw-in for the non-leaguers to score. The Stags spared their blushes when midfielder Paul Matthews equalised soon after, but within a minute Matlock had regained the advantage thanks to Nick Fenoughty again. At half time it was 2-1 to the part-timers.

An hour into the game Colin Foster brought some sanity to proceedings by leveling the tie with his head, but what happened next was a disaster of mammoth proportions. Matlock came blazing back in retaliation and Nick Fenoughty restored their lead. The game descended into farce with further goals for the part-timers, as every Stags fan held their head in disbelief. It was the club's first home defeat in almost a year and an embarrassing end to the Cup dream.

It was the era of David and Goliath style cup shocks, however. I remember screaming for the underdog as Leatherhead, from the Isthmian League, went 2-0 up against First Division Leicester City, only to lose 3-2 in a televised tie; when Blyth Spartans beat Stoke City to reach the fifth round before going out to Wrexham at Newcastle's St James's Park in front of 42,000; and when non-league Wimbledon held champions Leeds United to a draw at Elland Road, thanks to a penalty save by Dickie Guy. As a Leeds nut back then, relieved I was to see my heroes scrape through with a 1-0 win – courtesy of an own goal - in the replay at Selhurst Park.

8. Stags 2 Wolverhampton Wanderers 3
FA Cup Third Round, 7th January 1995

It was another case of so close but yet so far for Stags boss Andy King after this stirring cup tie at Field Mill. His team had secured the plum draw after beating Halifax Town in a replay and the home contingent in a crowd of almost 7,000 sensed a giant killing. Afterall, King's free-scoring young team knew no fear. They were cavalier in their approach and had the game's newest lethal weapon – a young black striker by the name of O'Neill Matthias Donaldson.

King plucked the willowy young marksman from obscurity. He had been struggling to make a breakthrough with neighbours Doncaster Rovers so their manager Sammy Chung sanctioned his to move to Field Mill on a month's loan. Seeing something in Donaldson that Chung definitely had not, King agreed a provisional fee of £15,000 if the loan spell proved successful. And it certainly did. Too successful, in fact!

Donaldson scored twice on his debut in a 7-1 win over Hereford United on Boxing Day and added two more in successive games against Scarborough and Barnet. Wolves had clearly under-estimated this new sensation, as they were powerless to prevent his seventh goal in five games just minutes into the tie. Field Mill was rocking, It was the sheer pace of Donaldson and co-striker Stewart Hadley that sent waves of panic through a surprisingly pedestrian Wolves defence, but moments later Simon Ireland – cup hero against Leeds United earlier in the season – unbelievably made it 2-0.

King was probably taking another satisfied drag of his trademark cigar when the First Division side hit back early in the second half to quieten down the Stags faithful. Wolves, driven forward by such quality as David Kelly, Gordon Cowans and recent million pound signing Don Goodman, began to get the upper hand as the Stags allowed themselves to defend too deep. Robbie Dennison equalised on the hour but it was Lee Mills who beat Darren Ward with a piledriver in the 70th minute to ruin all hopes of another big FA Cup run similar to those in the Sixties and Seventies.

For me, it wasn't the defeat as such that left me feeling so dejected, but the fact that my team had been on the verge of a big Cup upset. They had one foot in the Fourth Round draw, but blew it. King was rightfully proud of his team, and justifiably pointed out to me in an interview I recorded for 'Match of the Day' that "Graham Taylor must have been a very worried man." Unfortunately the clip was never used, which I found almost as disappointing as the result at the time. My TV career would have to wait.

9. Stags 1 Bury 5
Division Three, 28th October 1996

We've already considered Phil Stant's hero status during his time at Field Mill. Adored by the fans, he shot the club to that memorable promotion in 1991-92 with 26 goals. Four years later, he was back with his team Bury to play a starring role in one of the most bizarre games I ever saw.

Stant enjoyed a 90 minutes that any player could only dream of when facing a former club. Not only did he crash home four goals in a thumping 5-1 victory, but by the time his hat-trick was completed, the home fans were cheering his every touch. It was humiliating for a struggling Stags team devoid of goal power, but at the same time a measure of his undying popularity. It shouldn't have happened, and thankfully rarely does, but it was a tribute I know he found both humbling and emotional.

10. Torquay United v Stags - Abandoned
Division Three, 25th January 1997

Mansfield were going great guns under Steve Parkin, having notched straight wins over Hereford United, Hull City and Doncaster Rovers. Torquay were also enjoying a good spell, so the visiting squad was seriously pumped up for this eagerly-awaited clash at Plainmoor. It was an early start for the long trip to Devon and preparations for team and press were perfectly normal on a fine winter's afternoon– until Mother Nature intervened just 20 minutes before kick-off. That's when a mist began to loom in from the Babbacombe coast just a couple of hundred metres away from the stadium.

Referee Paul Rejer shared everyone's concerns when he inspected the pitch not once, but twice, before 3pm. Surely we hadn't ventured all the way to the Devon coast for nothing? Thankfully, he felt comfortable enough to give the game the go-ahead, but soon after that first whistle had been blown it became even more apparent that the sea fret was not retreating. In fact, conditions were getting worse by the minute and after consulting his linesmen Mr Rejer led the players off eight minutes before the break. As neither team could see the ball, never mind pass it properly, it was no surprise that the score was 0-0.

A 10-minute wait for some improvement proved a forlorn hope and the match was abandoned, leaving all the Mansfield contingent frustrated by such a long, wasted journey and a lost opportunity to keep the good run going. Parkin had no complaints. "The referee made the right decision," he admitted. But Torquay boss Kevin Hodges summed it up best. "I couldn't see the players and I don't think they could see the ball," he told me.

You might recall a similar situation at Field Mill a few years earlier when a cup tie against Preston was fogged off after little more than half an hour. That was equally frustrating, as I seem to remember Martin Tyler and Andy Gray being in attendance for a live Sky Sports broadcast. But at least it was only a 10 minute journey home for me.

CHAPTER 23

MY STAGS DREAM TEAM

As a Mansfield supporter for most of my life and correspondent for two decades, I have seen hundreds don the famous amber jersey, some with more distinction than others. But I couldn't complete this book without revealing my greatest ever Stags line up. That said, it has proven an arduous task and I don't mind admitting that I've poured over this chapter more than any other. So many fine players have prompted a myriad of memories, but here is my final 11, drawn painstakingly from the teams of the late Seventies, Eighties and Nineties. The following players may not be the most technically gifted, nor the ones who achieved the most in the game, but those who, for many reasons, made an indelible impression on me as first a fan, and later a journalist.

KEVIN HITCHCOCK (Goalkeeper)

Leaving the admirable Rod Arnold out of my team was one of the toughest decisions. Rod endeared himself to every Stags supporter during a distinguished 14-year career at Field Mill, and still holds the record for the most appearances in the club's green jersey – 515 to be precise. He was a true hero on the pitch and a great shot stopper, but the amazing exploits of my chosen custodian remain unequalled. Londoner Kevin Hitchcock wrote his name in Stags folklore with an unforgettable performance in that Wembley final of 1987, and the Stags faithful will always be indebted to him for those two amazing penalty shoot-out saves that helped the club taste glory.

'Hitchy' also excelled in the club's promotion from the old Fourth Division before that, and in the same season was named in the Third Division's PFA representative side. He also made the grade in the best league in the world, with Chelsea, of course, but was still awaiting his first team debut at Brian Clough's Nottingham Forest when Stags boss Ian Greaves brought him to Field Mill on loan in 1984. The young man from Canning Town quickly became a key cog in Greavesie's rebuilding programme and made his move permanent at the end of that season when the club invested £140,000 in his talents.

After 168 appearances, Hitchy made that dream move to Chelsea in 1988 for £250,000 and played 96 times for the Blues before following former manager Gianluca Vialli to Watford to become goalkeeping coach. He has since held similar positions at Blackburn, Manchester City, Fulham and Queen's Park Rangers. Interestingly, Kevin's son Tom made the grade at QPR as a striker.

SANDY PATE (Right Back)

Another difficult decision. One of my favourites Craig McKernon emerged from the successful Stags youth team that I reported on in my formative days, alongside the likes of Ian Stringfellow and Les Robinson, but only saw his career blossom when manager Greaves converted him from a midfielder to a full back. Though only 5ft 5ins tall, and slightly built, Craig read the game particularly well and had a good touch, but it was his blistering pace that set him apart from the rest and tempted Arsenal to fork out £200,000 for his services in 1989. Unfortunately knee problems blighted his time at Highbury and the Gloucestershire-born defender was never able to fulfill his promise.

Pate had no such problems, making 366 consecutive appearances in a Stags shirt. It's remarkable that he didn't miss a single match between 21st September 1968 and 9th August 1975! In total, Sandy played 471 times for his beloved Mansfield and became the ultimate clubman, captaining the side and commanding the upmost respect, and serving under no fewer than six different managers.

He was a mainstay in two promotion seasons and will always be remembered as one of the heroes of that legendary FA Cup giant killing of West Ham United in 1969. That was just before my time, but I've been blessed to get to know the great man in more recent years. – not only professionally but also as a member of his own pub team, the Traveller's Rest. Sandy was landlord of the Sutton-in-Ashfield establishment following several years behind the bar of the popular Portland Arms in Mansfield.

MARK KEARNEY (Left Back)

Another to be recruited by Greaves, Mark arrived at Field Mill from Everton in 1983 and must rate as one of the best free transfers in the club's long history. Like Hitchcock, he became an automatic choice in the club's promotion campaign in 1984 and was also a member of the Wembley-winning Freight Rover Trophy team of 1987, as a midfielder. Though also effective in midfield during his 303-game career at Field Mill, I remember Mark as a reliable defender with a sweet left foot who sweated blood for the amber jersey.

Indeed, it was a great testimony to his determination and dedication that he came back from a career-threatening injury during his time at Field Mill. I will never forget the shock waves that shook everyone in the stadium when Mark suffered a badly broken leg against Fulham on a midweek night in 1987. During his long rehabilitation, I visited him at his Mansfield home on several occasions and couldn't fail to be moved by his determination and commitment to the club at such a difficult time. Such was his stature that Greaves made the brave decision of awarding him a new contract to dispel any worries he may have had about his future in the game. Typically Mark repaid that gesture by making 100 or so more appearances for the club before joining Bury in 1991. He later had a spell at Telford United with former Stags boss George Foster before hanging up his boots in 1997. Since then Mark has held a number of coaching jobs and is still in the game today.

GEORGE FOSTER (Central Defender, Captain)

The central defensive positions proved to be the hardest for me to fill, given the club's tremendous tradition of producing back four lynchpins down the decades. Stuart Boam in the Sixties, locally-born Adrian Burrows and Mick Saxby in the late-Seventies, Northern Ireland international John McClelland, Worksop's Simon Coleman and another Wembley hero Tony Kenworthy were among the best.

Like Kearney, George joined Greaves at Field Mill on a free transfer and proved his worth on 373 occasions in a 10-year playing career at Mansfield. Even when he first arrived from Derby County lacking match practice, and carrying a few unwanted pounds, George immediately stamped his presence on the team and fitting it was that he lifted the silverware in that famous Wembley final of '87.

A success in the West Country with Plymouth Argyle between 1974 and 1982, he has to rank as one of the best value signings in Mansfield's long history and it was his combative, never-say-die approach that sets him apart from some steely names. But a pity it was that as a manager George never enjoyed the same popularity as he did as club captain, despite winning promotion. However, none of his persistent hecklers could ever deny that during a decade on the Field Mill pitch, Foster was a colossus, a true inspiration and the fiercest of competitors.

KEVIN BIRD (Central Defender)

The great Kevin Bird wore the amber shirt with distinction throughout 11 seasons, making over 400 appearances between 1972 and 1983. Doncaster Rovers had cast the young defender aside when Danny Williams offered him a trial at Field Mill, and it was a trial he passed with flying colours.

Uncompromising, he was the Tommy Smith or the Chopper Harris of the lower divisions and invariably stamped his presence on a game with an early firm tackle. Few got past Kevin, on the ground or in the air, but he could pick out a pass, too, and scored a catalogue of trademark goals from set pieces. His competitive spirit epitomised everything that was good about the club as it swept to two promotions in the space of two years in the mid-Seventies, and it is fitting that the function suite in the main grandstand at the new One Call Stadium carries his name.

PAUL HOLLAND (Central Midfield)

Such a crucial position in any team, filled by influential playmakers like Peter Morris in the Sixties, the late Gordon Hodgson in the Seventies, and John Matthews and Tony Lowery in the Eighties. But my shirt goes to a player whose ability to shape a game belied his tender years. I broke the story for the Chad when Paul, watched by his proud parents, signed schoolboy forms with the club. Among his generation, he was considered the 'special one', so it didn't come as a surprise when he made his debut for the Stags at the end of the 1990-91 season just ahead of his 18th birthday before going on to represent England at Under 21 level. In fact, I'm pretty sure he is the only 'Third Division' player to do so to this day.

A box-to-box competitor in the Bryan Robson mould, Lincolnshire-born Paul complemented his unquenchable desire with the ability to score goals that were usually spectacular, and often brave. He was a shining light in the 1992 promotion side, scoring vital goals against York City, Gillingham, Carlisle United and arch-rivals Chesterfield and deserved to play at a higher level with Sheffield United. It was a pity that his spell as manager at Field Mill ended in disappointing circumstances in 2008.

KEVIN KENT (Right Midfield)

'Kenty' wrote his name in Mansfield Town folklore when he swept home the only goal in open play in the Freight Rover Trophy Final. Indeed, it defined his six-year career at Field Mill. The euphoria that engulfed me when his low shot eluded the outstretched arm of Keith Waugh was the stuff of dreams.

Another young talent recruited by Greaves, Kent arrived in 1985 from Newport County, eager to establish a career that began at West Bromwich Albion. During his time with the Stags, he possessed that rare ability to change games and was wholly reliable – without doubt one of the most consistent performers who could always be relied upon to create a goal from the right wing, or even find the net himself when it mattered.

Kevin earned a move to his home town club Port Vale in 1991 in a part-exchange move involving Gary Ford. At Vale Park, he won more silverware in the Autoglass Trophy back at Wembley in 1993. Great company off the field of play, as well as dedicated on it, Kevin worked with me as a summariser on Radio Nottingham on a number of occasions so it was no surprise that he went on to do some media work towards the end of his career.

STEVE CHARLES (Left Midfield)

Sheffield-born Steve had gained considerable experience with his home city club The Blades and then Wrexham before joining the Stags for a bargain £15,000 in 1987. He made an instant impact, scoring 12 goals from midfield in his first season and became a mainstay in the side throughout the next four years.

'Charlie' gets into my team for several reasons: he was the definitive Mr Dependable, whose work rate was second to none. Like Holland, who later became a team mate, he was a true midfield dynamo, supporting his defence, stealing back the advantage and creating and scoring goals with some regularity. A smart guy with degrees in mathematics and marketing, he was also a natural athlete who would run his team mates into submission in pre-season training and was admired in the dressing room for his 'Duracell' constitution. Tucking into the left of my midfield, alongside Holland and opposite Kent, Steve gives my Dream Team a beautiful balance.

KEITH CASSELLS (Striker)

My team is built to attack, with three forwards who between them scored dozens of great goals for the club. Choosing my strikers was almost as difficult as filling those central defensive positions, but after great deliberation I've selected the greatest winger and two of the most lethal goal poachers of my own era.

Keith Cassells brings a touch of class to the line up. Another star of the Greaves reign, the potent number 10 quickly repaid his modest price tag by becoming leading scorer twice for the Stags. It was he who almost single-handedly set the tone for the club's promotion year in 1986 when he blasted a hat-trick past Hereford United in a 4-0 opening day win at Field Mill. Then, at the end of April, he fired two more past Hartlepool United to finally clinch their place in the old Third Division.

A thoroughly lovely guy on and off the field of play, 'Cass' also played his part in getting the Stags to Wembley in 1987, and covered every blade of the famous turf in the final. But my heart sank to my boots when he missed from the penalty spot in the shoot-out. Another 25,000 shared his agony, and how unjust it would have been had his failure from the spot cost the club their moment of glory.

RAY CLARKE (Centre Forward)

Imagine for a moment the partnership that Terry Eccles, Dave Syrett or Phil Stant would have forged with our predator Cassells ... Great centre forwards of their era, and all prolific scorers in their own right. But the number nine shirt must go to a player whose exploits at Field Mill sent his career international. Ray Clarke brought a certain glamour and flair to the club in those heady days of the Seventies.

The former Swindon Town front man fired Dave Smith's Stags to promotion in 1975 with 28 goals, and I was there to celebrate the majority of them from the terraces. As a fanatical 10-year-old, I reveled in his prowess in the box – particularly when he rounded off an unforgettable season with two goals amid a party atmosphere in that 7-0 rout of Scunthorpe United in the April of that year. He added another 24 goals the following season before earning a big-money move to Sparta Rotterdam. In those days, £90,000 was a hefty fee but that was topped twice when Brighton and then Newcastle United employed his sought-after talents.

JIMMY McCAFFREY (Winger)

Now I'm wrestling with my conscience. If I allow my heart to rule my head, then my original footballing hero Malcolm Partridge will be installed on the wing. However, with Kevin Kent already placed to deliver a threat from the right, my winger has been chosen to patrol the left touchline.

At just 5ft 7ins and asthmatic, Jimmy McCaffrey had challenges to overcome, but in my mind the Luton-born wide man became one of the most exciting players ever to don a Stags shirt. The roar of anticipation when Jimmy received the ball on the wing was deafening. It was a proven formula. Off he would dash, jinking down the channel and leaving the full back in his wake before delivering a pin-point cross for Clarke or Eccles to dispatch into the back of the net during that golden era in the mid-Seventies.

....

Strikers, more than players in any other position, conjure the most vivid memories among supporters, and I could dedicate another chapter to the magical moments provided by a succession of front men over the years. Young Scot Dave Caldwell possessed pace and an incisive finish, scoring 21 goals in 1983-4; Stant, who I've dedicated a chapter to, became a true hero in the early Nineties; and Steve Wilkinson fitted a similar bill in breaking club scoring records in the mid-Nineties, to name but three.

Ask Stags fans of an older generation to compile their star 11 and the majority would include legendary Sixties forward Ken Wagstaff. Ken's 34 and 29-goal returns came just before my birth, hence his exclusion from my personal Dream Team. I've also had the pleasure of Dudley Roberts' company on occasions, including when I hosted a tribute evening at Field Mill to commemorate the 40th anniversary of the famous FA Cup victory over West Ham United a few years ago. Like Ken, Dudley made his contribution to the Stags hall of fame before I was old enough to become a devoted fan, but he too would rightfully make it onto many shortlists.

CHAPTER 24

A RACING CERTAINTY

Having achieved my lifelong ambition to be a football commentator, the chance to move into television as a horse racing presenter in 2002 was too appealing to dismiss. Horses, and particularly racing, was a passion that had been smouldering inside me since childhood and I had been working hard to push my career in that direction for several years. My first breakthrough into the racing media came in 1994 when, as a freelance, I made a speculative phone call to the weekly form paper, Raceform Update. The editor, a charming man by the name of Len Bell, offered me some shifts at their Eccles offices in Manchester, based largely on my experience as a sub-editor and writer. It was a small office, with old wooden desks and word processors. Len headed a small team that included a young trainee called Gideon Brooks, who later made a name for himself as a sports writer at the Daily Express.

The journeys were long and arduous but I enjoyed writing the 'Longbow' race previews and soon convinced Len to give me my own weekly All-Weather racing column. Racing on sand was in its relative infancy in those days and a section dedicated to it was a definite niche. I had adopted a keen interest in the All-Weather since one of the first tracks of its kind had been put down at my local course, Southwell, and sensed an opportunity to fashion myself into a specialist in the subject. Very quickly the column began to attract an enthusiastic following, so to further build my reputation as a budding All-Weather expert I published the first of a series of annual books previewing the forthcoming winter season. The 'All-Weather Guide' featured interviews with trainers, horses to follow and facts about the country's three All-Weather tracks at the time. Adverts and sponsorship from bookmakers financed the production and the first guide sold well enough to justify repeating it.

Some years earlier I had met top National Hunt jockey Steve Smith Eccles, who was born and bred in Pinxton on the Derbyshire border. Steve became the first jockey to have a benefit year and I organised a dinner for him at Mansfield's Civic Centre. It was a successful night, with eminent racing journalist John Sexton a guest speaker and ITV commentator Graham Goode performing an auction. Valuable contacts were being forged. My friendship with 'The Ecc' opened another door when I landed the job of ghost writing his regular column on Teletext. And it was Steve who was instrumental in getting me a guest slot on the original Racing Channel to promote my first book.

My own column dedicated to All-Weather racing was soon established on

Teletext and suddenly I was becoming widely acknowledged as the leading media authority on the sport. Pundit appearances followed on the Racing Channel's 'Racing News' programme on the Sky Sports platform, working alongside such esteemed presenters as the great Richard Pitman, Sky Sports News's Alex Hammond and leading commentator Ian Bartlett. More successful editions of the All-Weather Guide followed, and suddenly racing journalism was becoming as big a part of my career as football. Though still entrenched in the 'beautiful game', and enjoying following the fortunes of the Stags, an exciting new career path was beginning to emerge and I passed many a Saturday morning journey to an away game with my head buried in the Sporting Life.

By the new millennium I had given up competitive riding in local events and competitions, due to work commitments and the demands of a young family, and turned my attention to buying and syndicating racehorses. I had reveled in every minute I spent showjumping, eventing and bloodhounding on my horse Dancer, a thoroughbred-Hanoverian cross I bought when I climbed back into the saddle in my mid-Twenties, but time was at a premium and equestrianism demanded much more commitment than I could afford to give it. Buying racehorses was the perfect compromise. It allowed me to maintain my hands-on interest in bloodstock, but brought more important benefits along with it. The horses I was buying – in training in those days with Edwinstowe handler Roy Bowring – were winning races. I had a natural eye for a winner and my success as an owner was enhancing my credibility in the racing media.

In early 2002, a phone call out of the blue invited me to audition for a new dedicated racing channel on the Sky Sports platform that was to be called 'Attheraces'. Competition for places on the team of about 12 presenters was fierce, to say the least, but my screen test went well enough to impress a panel including Channel 4 Racing's creator Andrew Franklin. Within days, I had been offered my first regular job in television – news that excited me even more than my call up by Radio Nottingham 13 years earlier. Weeks later, my coverage of Mansfield's promotion drive would bring to an end my career as a Stags correspondent and commentator, but a new adventure was about to commence.

The Stags did indeed clinch promotion and commentating on their final day victory over Carlisle United was an appropriate way to hang up my lip mic after 13 seasons and those 650 matches for the local BBC station. Soon, reporting on live horse racing took me all over Britain, and on occasions into Southern Ireland. I was previewing races, analysing the form and interviewing all the stars of the sport, from Frankie Dettori to the late Sir Henry Cecil. It was thrilling at times, but also mentally exhausting. Live television was a new experience for me. I was out of my comfort zone, but the spontaneity of live radio proved a good grounding and I soon got to grips with the demands.

Along with the daily racing coverage on the digital channel came a 'Lunchtime Trifecta' programme for Channel 4, the summer evening 'Winning Post' on Sky Sports and an appearance on Channel 4 Racing's 'The Morning Line' and afternoon show from Lingfield Park. There was also the opportunity to present Royal Ascot from the studio. In media terms, I was now at the forefront of a fast-moving seven-day-a-week industry, working alongside such big names as John McCririck, Mike Cattermole and Derek Thompson, and loving every minute of it. Being terrorised by a streaker on live television alongside McCririck still rates as my most hysterical TV moment.

More high profile days on television followed each season, including the world's oldest classic, the St Leger Stakes at Doncaster, and the Yorkshire track's famous cavalry charge the Lincoln Handicap. I was also dispatched to County Tipperary in leafy Ireland to record a special feature programme about the world-famous Coolmore Stud, profiling great stallions such as Sadler's Wells and Montjeu. The All-Weather, meanwhile, was still a speciality and I was widely acknowledged as the leading authority on the winter code. I was living the dream all over again. Football remained close to my heart, but the opportunity to professionally pursue my lifelong passion for racing through the medium of live television was tremendously exciting.

On the racetrack, my success as an owner continued on turf as well as on sand. Treason Trial won a notable handicap at York two years running, while little sprinter Lady Protector – bought for just 3,400 guineas at the Newmarket sales – won three races, and was placed in a big handicap at Glorious Goodwood on Sussex Stakes day. Tyzack completed five consecutive wins, four of them at my local track Southwell, and Mind Alert scored twice there to enhance my reputation as an All-Weather expert. In 2003, I even completed the qualifications required to become a racehorse trainer.

A few years later, it was another sprint filly Wibbadune, again a bargain buy, who became my winning-most horse, landing six wins inside a year. But my proudest moment as an owner was seeing my orange and purple checked silks carried to a high profile victory at the Champions' Meeting at Newmarket in 2005. Coconut Squeak, a filly I bought from Doncaster Sales for 12,000 guineas and retained a half share in, sprung a 50-1 surprise in a Listed race to give me my biggest ever success. She had only won a lowly claimer when the hammer fell in my direction but became a prize asset when she was sold to stud a year later. Thanks to the excellent trainers I worked with, I reached a proud total of 40 winners as an owner – achieved by 20 different horses all bought in the bargain basement.

Going racing with my parents as a small boy, as we did on many occasions, I could never have imagined myself becoming a successful racehorse owner, never mind a racing presenter on television. But I will never take for granted how blessed I have been to pursue for a living not just one but two of my biggest passions in life - football and horse racing - over three wonderful decades. Getting paid for doing a dream job is indeed a privilege, but one that demands a great deal of hard work, determination and an undying will to succeed.

INDEX